A 1970s Teenager

A 1970s Teenager

From Bell-Bottoms to Disco Dancing

Simon Webb

The
History
Press

First published 2013

The History Press
The Mill, Brimscombe Port
Stroud, Gloucestershire, GL5 2QG
www.thehistorypress.co.uk

© Simon Webb, 2013

The right of Simon Webb to be identified as the Author
of this work has been asserted in accordance with the
Copyrights, Designs and Patents Act 1988.

British Library Cataloguing in Publication Data.
A catalogue record for this book is available from the British Library.

ISBN 978 0 7524 8815 8

Typesetting and origination by The History Press
Printed in Great Britain

Contents

	Acknowledgements	6
	Introduction	7
1.	Music	13
2.	Communications	41
3.	Fashion	63
4.	Alcohol and Drugs	81
5.	Sex	95
6.	Getting Around	109
7.	Politics	129
8.	Television	139
9.	School	145
10.	Work	153
11.	Belongings	159
12.	Relaxing	167
13.	The Generation Gap	172
14.	The Alternative Society	180
15.	We're All Teenagers Now	184
16.	The Teenage Tribes of the 1970s	188

Acknowledgements

Thank you to the following people: Chris Arthur, Terry Barlow, Mary A. Barker, Paul Clarke, Katherine Cassidy, Geoffrey C. Feldman, David Ford, Esther M. Hannigan, Pat Howard, Theresa O. Littlestone, Gillian V. Pettitt, Sarah P. Moran, Martin O'Connell, Mick Parker, Polly Reynolds, K.A. Silverstone, Maria T. Valentine, Christopher Walker, and Nina Webb.

Introduction

For those who were teenagers then, the 1970s must surely have been the most exciting decade there has ever been. It is fashionable now to be dismissive about many of the visual features of those years, dismissing it as 'The decade style forgot', but at the time it all seemed so fantastically vibrant and colourful. This book is a celebration of the 1970s; 'the good, the bad and ugly.' There was, after all, more to those times than just *Abigail's Party*, the *Bay City Rollers*, platform shoes, and flared trousers.

I do not believe that there has ever been a better time to be a teenager than the seventies! It was brash and noisy, the fashions were ghastly, but it was all tremendous fun. Our music was being heard everywhere, those of us who were working always seemed to have plenty of money and the atmosphere of crisis which permeated the whole decade served only to make it seem richer and more exotic. The various strikes and riots, the IRA attacks on the mainland, the Winter of Discontent and Thatcher being elected; even at the time I knew that we were living through a momentous period of change. (Polly Reynolds)

Although they could not have fully known it at the time, teenagers of the 1970s were growing to maturity on the very cusp of the transition from the post-war years to the modern world. This was when the twentieth century began to gear up and ready itself for the change to the twenty-first century. At the beginning of the decade, the technology in use had changed little since the end of Queen Victoria's reign; slide rules, mechanical typewriters, telephones, clockwork watches and even gramophones were still in use. By 1979, the electronic revolution had begun and there were digital watches, pocket calculators, Walkmans and even the first personal computers.

> I was born in 1960 and the changes that I saw taking place during my teenage years, from 1973-9, were absolutely dizzying. It was like watching the birth of the modern world. Every year there was something new. I remember seeing a video recorder in somebody's house for the first time, using a push button telephone instead of one with a dial, my first digital watch, and computer games in amusement arcades and pubs. Although at that age you don't recognise the full significance of what you are seeing, I realised that the world was changing very fast. (Paul Clarke)

Teenagers who grew up over the course of the 1970s were witness to these changes. A thirteen-year-old attending school in 1970 would have been using a slide rule; by the time he was twenty he would probably have had a pocket calculator. In 1970, most televisions were black and white; by 1980, not only were colour televisions more commonplace, but one could even record pro-grammes to watch later. Computer games like Space Invaders were also making an appearance at this time.

Those whose teenage years spanned the 1970s saw more changes taking place than any other generation since the Industrial Revolution.

> Of course, young people adapt much more easily to change than old people. There was so much happening in the seventies, from the end of pounds, shillings and pence in 1971, to the first woman Prime Minister in 1979. I know my parents felt a little bewildered at the pace of change and my grandparents could not keep track of things at all. Because I was a teenager I had nothing to compare it to, but my parents had seen slow and steady changes and gradual development from the twenties through to the sixties. Suddenly, the pace accelerated and things were changing faster and faster. You had no sooner seen about computer games or portable calculators on *Tomorrow's World*, than they were in the shops or people's homes. It was a great time to be young! (Terry Barlow)

The term 'teenager' was not an invention of the 1970s; the expression dates back to the late 1940s. Pop music had been around since the 1950s and so too had various other features of 1970s teenage life. However, the fads, fashions and foibles of teenagers changed during those years from being footnotes in the news to becoming a dominant force in British culture. This was when the cult of youth began in this country and being young, or at least behaving as though one were young, became, for some, something to covet.

> When I was a kid in the sixties, my father even used to wear a collar and tie on the beach. By the time the eighties arrived, he was wearing jeans at the weekend. I could see that people his age were becoming more informal in their

dress and it struck me then that it was because they were
becoming a little wistful that they were not themselves
young any more. Of course, I do exactly the same thing
myself today, sharing clothes with my younger daughter.
I suppose it would be fair to say that at the age of fifty,
I don't want to grow up myself. (Anon)

The technology at the start of the 1970s had, essentially,
remained unchanged for many decades and so too had
the way that the average person dressed. At the end of the
1960s, only a teenager or person in their early twenties
would have worn a pair of blue jeans in public; by 1980,
even middle-aged men were wearing jeans and leaving
their shirts unbuttoned. Photographs of families relaxing
on the beach in the 1950s and '60s show men wearing
sports jackets and even collars and ties. This would have
been unthinkable by the 1980s. The 1970s saw a relaxation of the dress codes that had held sway since the end
of the First World War. It was the decade when everybody
wanted to appear young; when being a teenager was suddenly an admirable ambition, even for men and women in
their forties.

It was pretty embarrassing when my parents decided to
become more 'with it', as they would have put it. Something
that you always notice about parents when they try to act
young is that their use of slang is often a bit out of style.
Beatniks in the fifties might have been 'with it', but to hear
my father using the phrase in the late seventies was a little
bit of an anachronism. Anyway, they began to listen to
music like ABBA and take an interest in what young people
were doing and saying. I think now that they felt that teenagers were having all the fun and so they should get into the

swing of things. I noticed in the pub at that time that you would see more and more middle-aged men hoping to look young and 'with it'. (David Ford)

The division between the various stages in life definitely began to become blurred for the first time during the late seventies. Before that, you were a schoolchild, then a young man or woman, followed by becoming middle aged and then old. At each stage in the process, there were accepted styles of dress, clothing, hairstyle and behaviour. For example, middle-aged women had their hair permed, rather than hanging long and loose. Old women had white hair, also permed. Young men might wear more casual clothes, but right up to the beginning of the seventies, middle-aged men were expected to be a bit more conservative. By the time you were an old man, which happened in those days at about the age of sixty, you would be wearing a collar and tie, even on a picnic! All this faded away as the seventies progressed.

 Older women were allowing their hair to be long and natural, middle-aged men were wearing jeans and open-necked shirts; the divisions between the ages were breaking down and older people wanted to look as much like teenagers as they dared; not all of them, of course, but it was certainly a noticeable trend. (Polly Reynolds)

For some years, the term 'pop music' had been used in a pejorative sense to denote the type of light music enjoyed by the young. By the 1970s it was being heard everywhere and enjoyed by all ages. Parents were as likely to enjoy listening to Simon and Garfunkel or ABBA as their children were, a trend which has continued to this day.

Looking back at the sixties, when I was growing up, I do remember that most television programmes had people speaking with very clear, what we would now call 'posh', accents and the background music was likely to be a string quartet or chamber orchestra. Some time during the seventies that all began to change and you would hear guitar music and modern stuff. It was as though the television producers made a conscious decision sometime around 1975 that they wanted their programmes not to sound so old-fashioned and that a good way of emphasising this was to have popular music instead of classical or baroque. It was all to do with sounding younger and more modern. (Paul Clarke)

Throughout the 1970s, music was, in a sense, the social glue that held teenage groups together, much as it is today.

1

Music

In the 1970s, music was the binding agent which helped to keep members of different teenage groups, or 'tribes', together. Teenagers were fanatically partisan about the style of music they favoured and even the individual artistes within the genre. It was not enough to like your own type of music; you had to actively dislike the music associated with rival teenage groups. To be eclectic in one's musical tastes would, at best, invite ridicule and could even amount to social suicide. The biker whose friends were into Black Sabbath or Deep Purple would never in a million years dare to mention that he quite liked some of Donny Osmond's songs! It would be almost as bad as a hippy admitting to his comrades that he was partial to Mantovani.

> We turned up unexpectedly at this guy's house one day, in around the mid-seventies. We surprised him while he was listening to an Engelbert Humperdinck record on his parent's stereo! It took him a year or so to live this down and it was something we used to bring up at odd moments whenever we were discussing music. He was never allowed to forget it.
> (K.A. Silverstone)

Some teenage groups were more open about this sort of thing than others, hippies in particular. For example, they could freely enjoy both Simon and Garfunkel and Led Zeppelin, but even within this group there were limits; it would have been going too far to tell people that you played your sister's David Cassidy LPs from time to time. Talking about popular music, reading about the musicians in magazines and watching their performances, either on television or in real life, was a big part of the group identity of young people.

There were a number of different and distinct styles of popular music when I was a teenager. There was a sort of snobbishness about which you favoured. Those who liked heavy rock like Black Sabbath would be a little 'sneery' about gentle stuff like James Taylor or Joni Mitchell, say. Those who liked Carole King would feel that their tastes were superior to somebody who liked ABBA and so on. Occasionally there was crossover from one type of music to another, but often teenagers were insular and conservative when it came to other people's music. (Anon)

The music we listened to was an important part of who we were. Some of the lyrics seemed to speak directly to us and we felt that whoever wrote those things had a lot in common with us. Now, although my tastes ran to bands like The Who, I happen to know that my little sister had exactly the same idea about this when she was listening to her Donny Osmond records. Perhaps this is a bit like good poetry, it comes across as being personal, even though the man who wrote it might have been dead for centuries. So I listened to songs that said things like: 'I've seen the needle and the damage done, a little part of it in everyone, but every junky's like the setting sun', and it would make me think about some of the drug users I had known. My sister listened to 'Puppy Love' and felt just the same; it spoke to her. (Geoffrey C. Feldman)

In the days before downloads and streaming, the acquisition of music was an important part of many teenager's lives; it was not (as is often the case these days) a solitary activity but a communal enterprise. Friends would visit each other and sit in a bedroom listening to an album. This would be done while leafing through fan magazines, with posters of the singer or band looking down on them from the wall.

> The girls that I hung round with from school used to meet round each others' houses and just sit in bedrooms listening to David Cassidy or Donny Osmond. There were no videos then and so we used to do the next best thing. Sitting on the floor or laying on the bed with a record playing, the walls nearly always covered with posters, while we looked at magazines containing more black and white photographs. I don't know why, but nearly every bed had a candlewick bedspread in those days; you never seem to see them these days. (Sarah P. Moran)

Today, nearly every teenager can access any song required with the click of a mouse and it can then be listened to alone or sent electronically to friends in a split second. In the 1970s, buying and sharing music was a physical act which required interaction with other people at every stage of the process. Buying a record would entail a trip to a shop. You might have had a chance to stand in an open booth to listen to the record first. Record shops were places to meet friends and talk about the latest music; even if you had no money to buy anything, they were a free place to hang out and chat.

Having bought your record and taken it home to listen to
again and again on a record player or, if you were lucky, a
stereo system, you might wish to lend it to a friend.

There was a record shop where we all used to go on Saturday
mornings. You could ask to listen to a record in one of the
booths. These were not closed off and more than one person
could squeeze in. The owner used to get a bit irritable, telling
us that it wasn't a youth club and that if we weren't going to
buy anything could we make room for those who were. It
was the whole thing, looking through the racks of records
together, talking about the singers and so on. It was how
I spent most of my Saturday mornings during 1971 and '72.
We couldn't often afford LPs and even buying single 45s was
not something we did every week. (Polly Reynolds)

Talking face-to-face with friends about music was something
of a feature of my life in those days. I know teenagers today,
who watch loads of clips on YouTube of their favourite
bands, but watching any music in the seventies simply had
to be a group activity; either you watched them on the television or at the cinema in films like *Woodstock*, or sometimes
at live concerts. This idea of watching a band play on your
own would have been a very strange one in those days.
Listening to music was a shared experience too, whether on
the radio or stereo; it was part of the thing. This business
now, where each person has a set of earphones plugged into
their head and they alone can hear the music, still looks a bit
odd to me. I was on the tube recently and there was a group
of girls, aged fifteen or sixteen. Two of them had earphones
in and the others were looking at their mobiles. There was
no shared sense of being a group at all. In my day we would
have been chattering away and sharing our thoughts. (Anon)

Lending records to friends was a whole activity in itself. It would often involve getting on the bus with the LP or single, going up to somebody's bedroom to listen to it together, while perhaps gazing at a poster of the singer on the wall. It must be borne in mind that listening to these analogue recordings while looking at still photographs was pretty much the only way of experiencing a singer or pop group in those days. Few could afford to own many records and so lending and borrowing was very common. These vinyl records were delicate though and had to be cleaned carefully and treated with respect. Friendships had been forever destroyed by somebody borrowing a Donny Osmond LP and returning it with a scratch, marring for all time his soul-searing rendition of 'Puppy Love'.

> I lent a close friend my favourite album, 'Ladies of the Canyon' by Joni Mitchell. When she returned it, it was in a dreadful state. She had obviously left it lying around out of the cover. In addition to a few little scratches, there was fluff and dust on it that could only have been picked up from a carpet. It is impossible to explain to the youth of today what a serious matter that was. I certainly couldn't afford to buy a new copy just like that and in fact this particular record had been a birthday present. Our friendship never really recovered. (Katherine Cassidy)

> The whole thing about music at that time was how ephemeral it was. You might see a singer on television and then that performance would be gone forever. The only reliable way of hearing a song again was by means of records or tapes. Lending these to each other was a physical operation and also a social interaction with friends. One actually had to lug the album from A to B and then have a conversation,

face-to-face. This is something which, to me, does not appear
to take place quite so much with teenagers today. Much of
their connection, not only in sharing music, is taking place in
cyberspace now. The new ways of listening to and acquiring
music are making it possible to see and hear practically any
singer or group at any time, but it is no longer a joint enterprise for teenagers in the way it once was. (K.A. Silverstone)

If one wanted to see the singer in person then, short of the
occasional concert, there was only one way to do it and
that was by watching them on television. In the days before
video this could be a tricky business, as it was necessary to
commandeer the family television set for half an hour on
Thursday evenings to watch *Top of the Pops*. But suppose
that one's mother and father wanted to watch something
themselves on a Thursday evening? This could be a disaster and precipitate tantrums and hysteria, particularly if a
singer was making a special appearance. Just imagine, David
Cassidy is about to sing his latest hit and your mum and dad
want to watch *It Ain't Half Hot Mum* on the other side!

I remember that on one occasion the Osmonds were on *Top
of the Pops* in 1973 and I was desperate to watch them sing
'Let Me In'. But no, my father wanted to watch some play
on BBC 2 and no matter how much I pleaded and begged
he remained adamant. Everybody I knew was watching the
Osmonds that November night except for me. I stormed up
to my bedroom in tears and felt that this was the cruellest
and most unjust thing that had ever happened since the
world began. (Sarah P. Moran)

Watching *Top of the Pops* was never a real pleasure when
I was fourteen or fifteen. My parents were pretty good about

letting me take over the TV at that time every Thursday, but neither of them could ever restrain themselves from making comments of the 'Gawd, you can't tell if it's a boy or a girl!' or 'Blimey, what a racket!' variety. It sounds silly now, but this sort of thing used to ruin the programme for me. My father in particular used to make jokes about my favourite singers or just stand there shaking his head in a sort of mime show. I would far rather have been able to watch it all by myself, but I could hardly have expected as a fourteen-year-old to be able to order my parents from the family living room. (Paul Clarke)

This situation, where one has to watch a screen at one particular time on a certain day or risk missing the event completely, is something which may seem incomprehensible to some teenagers today. They are able to view clips of their favourite singers on YouTube and DVDs, able to record programmes, and watch shows on BBC iPlayer and other modern media.

You would wait all week if some favourite band like the Bay City Rollers was due to appear on *Top of the Pops*. I have tried to explain to some young people that I know how important an event it was to see these stars actually performing on the screen, but I honestly don't think that they get it. Why would they want to sit in the same room as their mum and dad to listen to and watch some popular band? The state of affairs now is so utterly different. If they want to see any singer performing, all they have to do is Google it and they can track down film of a performance in a matter of seconds. At risk of sounding like an old fogy, I think that they miss a lot like this. There is no pleasurable anticipation, no counting off the days until it's time for the show. (Esther M. Hannigan)

An important reason for watching *Top of the Pops*, quite apart from the enjoyment of seeing your favourite group perform, was that this became itself a social event the following day at school or in the pub. 'Did you see so and so last night? Wasn't he dreamy? I must get that single on Saturday.' The inability to record and play back television programmes like *Top of the Pops* meant that magazines and newspapers aimed at teenagers were an important way of keeping up with your chosen singers, even when you couldn't actually watch them.

> If you didn't read *Melody Maker*, you would soon find yourself being out of touch. It was the only way of finding out when an album was being released, the dates of concerts, news about the bands and all the rest of it. Now you would only need to Google some singer's name and you would be able to find out everything about him. Some of them Tweet, which means that you might know five minutes later what he had for breakfast. Forty years ago though, all the information came from papers like *Melody Maker*. Some people belonged to fan clubs and they would get magazines or newsletters about particular singers or bands, but for the rest of the time you had to rely upon the papers. (Mary A. Barker)

Melody Maker and *New Musical Express* were read each week for news of the pop and rock scene. Magazines like *Jackie* gave girls the personal information that they required about the singers upon whom they had crushes. Take the 28th June 1975 issue, for example. It included a long piece about Elton John, telling about his relationship with his mother, how he gets depressed sometimes and how he relaxes – all the little details that teenage girls wanted to know, except, of course, the crucial fact that he was gay!

My father used to crack jokes about Elton John being gay
and I found it really upsetting. His newspaper had apparently carried a piece which hinted about it. I think it was to
the effect that Elton John was known by a girl's name among
some circle of friends, Beryl I think. I know it sounds silly,
but the thought that he might be gay was terribly upsetting,
because of course it wrecked my fantasy of Elton John meeting me and then falling madly in love with me. It would be
hard to imagine a singer today managing to keep something
like that off the internet for long! (Polly Reynolds)

Today, any information about the private life of any pop
singer spreads like wildfire across the internet. It is impossible to control personal details about anybody in the
public eye. During the 1970s though, it was still possible to
keep the lid on scandals and unconventional or unsavoury
aspects of a singer's life. Despite the fan clubs and interviews in magazines like *Jackie*, fans were very much kept
in the dark about their idols. Some even married without
it becoming public knowledge, something which would be
exceedingly hard in this day and age.

Parents would often dismiss any music being listened
to by their teenage children as being a terrible racket,
although this did change a bit towards the later years of
the decade.

My father used to claim that he couldn't actually hear
any music when I had one of my records on. He said that
it just sounded like a noise to him and that all he could
hear was the boom, boom, boom of the bass. Another
of his complaints was that he couldn't hear the words
and that when he could, the lyrics didn't seem to make
any sense. It is quite funny in retrospect, because I now

realise that he was trying to wind me up and succeeded
very well. I used to get furiously angry about what I saw
as his philistinism. (Esther M. Hannigan)

Parents' claiming that the music their children listen to is
noisy and unmelodic was not something which began in
the 1970s. It could be that some of the most treasured classical music was once dismissed by the older generation of
the time as being a frightful racket.

I was a great fan of James Taylor and used to listen to him in
my room all the time when I was sixteen. My father would
sometimes come in and listen for a minute or two and then
ask why he always sounded so gloomy. He made the same
comment about some of my other favourites, Neil Young for
instance. He used to reminisce about some of the bands of
his youth in the thirties and tell me that they always sounded
a lot more cheerful. I have listened lately to an awful lot of
the music that I enjoyed from say nineteen seventy-one to
seventy-five and in fact I see now that my father had a point;
it does sound a little gloomy. The singers always sound as
though things aren't going right for them. I suppose since
that's how teenagers feel a lot of the time anyway, music like
that is calculated to appeal to them. (Theresa O. Littlestone)

Music Technology

When the decade began, most teenagers hoping to listen
to the music of their choice were restricted to a record
player that was usually mono. Vinyl records were what
everybody listened to, but by the end of the decade cassette
tapes were also fairly common, although records were

what most people wanted. There was something satisfying about a large, cardboard LP case which the small plastic cassettes did not have.

> When you bought an LP, you had a tangible object, a possession. Everything about it was satisfying. The cover art, the fact that there were likely to be photographs of the singer, possibly the lyrics printed on the sleeve. My children download music all the time now, but they don't actually *have* anything. My collection of albums in some way defined who I was. Anybody looking through them could have told a lot about me, just from seeing those records. You had to think carefully about which records you were going to buy, because of course you couldn't afford all the music you would like to have available to play. This made us think more about our music; it was not just a free commodity the way it is now for kids on the internet. (David Ford)

> There was something pleasurable about buying an album. They were large, they were substantial and you felt that you had obtained value for the £1.50 or £2 which you handed over. There was something richly fulfilling about carrying home an LP and knowing that it was now yours and that you could listen to the songs on it as often as you wished to do so. The thing to remember is that most teenagers did not have all that many LPs and you could get a little tired of hearing the same ones all the time. It was a real treat to have a new lot of songs to hear on demand. This is not a pleasure that most teenagers have today. They have unlimited access to music, as much as they want really. Most people have something like Spotify, and even for those who don't, they are always sending each other music or watching it on YouTube. (Terry Barlow)

Stereos were expensive and usually owned by parents rather than their children. Since these were generally installed in the living room or lounge, and considering that most parents did not want to listen to their teenage offspring's pop music, this usually meant relying on a record player in the bedroom.

> In the late 1950s, my parents bought a record player. Then, ten years later, they bought a proper stereo system. I inherited the old record player, which I had in my bedroom. It was a pretty primitive thing really, it was just mono. Even so, I thought it wonderful that I could actually sit in my room and choose what I listened to. I got a Saturday job after that, mainly so that I could afford to buy records. Simon and Garfunkel, James Taylor, Joni Mitchell; my friends used to come round and we would just sit there in my room listening to our favourite singers and talking. This was the biggest part of our social lives in the seventies, just sitting in each other's bedrooms and listening to old record players. (Nina Webb)

Putting a record on to play demanded surgical precision, in order to not scratch it. The needle had to be lowered slowly and carefully onto precisely the right place. On the more expensive record players and stereos, this could be done automatically and the arms themselves were finely balanced, but on the sort of old model to be found in the average teenager's bedroom, the operation had to be carried out by hand. Sometimes, you might want to listen to a particular track in the middle of an album and this required even more finely gauged movements. The problem was that, in contrast to today's digital technology, the piece of music represented by a record was really a one-off. Few teenagers could afford to buy replacements for records if they were damaged and so they took good care of them.

Taking care of records was practically a hobby in itself. You had to make quite sure to put them back in the paper sleeve and then the cardboard cover. I had a special felt brush that was used to remove dust from records and also cleaning fluids. The stylus had to be changed pretty regularly too otherwise your records could get damaged by one that was too worn. (Geoffrey C. Feldman)

You forget how much care you had to take of vinyl records. Most of the gadgets that kids use today to listen to music – their mobiles and MP3 players – are pretty robust and can be left around. Not so with vinyl records. They quite literally used to attract dirt through static electricity. You had to use a special cloth or brush to attract the dirt back out of the grooves. Handling a record was like dealing with some priceless and irreplaceable artefact. You had to hold them by the edge, heaven forbid that you should allow them to get finger marks on the surface. If you left the thing out of its case it would be sure to get a scratch, which could make it unplayable. Since these were expensive items, you took great care of them. An ordinary album in the mid-seventies cost £2, which would be the equivalent of maybe £20 or £25 today. Your record collection was worth something. At a pinch, if you were really hard up, you could always flog a few albums. (Gillian V. Pettitt)

By the end of the 1970s, the price of stereos had fallen and they became more accessible to young people. Portable cassette players were on the market by 1970, but they were not particularly cheap either. A stereo system on which to play cassettes cost around £70 in 1970, the equivalent to perhaps £1,000 in modern terms, way beyond the reach of most teenagers.

> Something which those who grew up in the age of digital
> music will never understand is how fragile our old music was.
> I remember that my James Taylor album got scratched, right
> at the beginning of 'Fire and Rain'. This was a major disaster;
> I couldn't afford to go out and buy another copy. We had to
> take great care of our records, they were all but irreplaceable.
> My own children download stuff all the time, the idea of
> treasuring a record is quite alien to them. (Nina Webb)

In today's era of universal access to music, this can be
a quite hard concept to grasp. It explains why it was so
vital for the young person to be allowed to watch television programmes like *Top of the Pops*. The closest thing
to downloading music from the internet came in the latter
part of the 1970s, when cassette recorders became more
common. It was then possible to copy records onto tapes
and to also record radio programmes. This could be a
nerve-racking business though. Unless you had a special
connection to the stereo, you would have to put the tape
recorder's microphone near to the record player and record
it that way. It was almost a certainty that under such circumstances, one's mother would be sure to knock on the
door during the recording to announce that tea was ready.

> I remember taping albums in my bedroom. I suppose that
> these were the first illegal downloads. We certainly knew that
> it was against the law to copy music and circulate it in this way.
> One person would have a record and then we would borrow
> it and tape it onto cassette. The quality was not brilliant, but it
> was better than nothing. I had a microphone for my portable
> cassette player, but only a record player to record from. This
> meant setting the record up to play and then positioning the
> microphone near the speaker – primitive stuff indeed. (Anon)

One modern invention that was released at the end of the decade was the personal stereo, the Walkman. These were hugely expensive to begin with, but the novelty of walking down the street, privately listening to your own music, was seen to be unbelievably cool at the time. In the 1960s, teenagers used to walk along holding a transistor radio to their ear, now they used earphones and the enjoyment of music was changing from being a social activity to a private pleasure.

> There were transistor radios with little earplugs way back in the sixties, but the idea of having both ears closed up like that and listening to something which nobody else could hear was a bit strange. Of course, at home you could clamp a gigantic pair of headphones on, but that was not common. The Walkman was revolutionary in that it meant that the music you listened to was for you alone. It was not intended to be shared. Today, it is very common to see people with earphones in listening to MP3 players, but back in 1979 the idea was radical in the extreme. (Paul Clarke)

During this period, teenagers took enormous care of the devices which played their music. A broken record player would have been a major disaster for many teenagers. Things like cassette players and stereos were very expensive and were the kind of thing that one would have to save up for, or perhaps receive as a birthday or Christmas present. There was certainly not an endless stream of such gadgets, as there is today.

> I had a cassette player in 1972, before the price fell dramatically and they became something that everybody had laying around. Anyway, I used it for taping music and playing cassettes. One day, disaster struck. I spilled a cup of tea all over it and it stopped working. This was a terrible thing to happen,

because there was no question of just going out and buying a new one straight away. Until I had saved up enough for a new one, that was it; I just couldn't play any of my music. My own children lose or break MP3 players, phones and so on all the time. They always seem to find a way to replace them though. (Chris Arthur)

I remember buying my first stereo in 1976. I was eighteen and had just moved into a place of my own, which was a bedsit. The one thing that I simply had to have to make life bearable was a stereo. They were pretty expensive, so I bought a fairly basic system with a deck and speakers for £45. That was a week's wages for me at the time and I only managed it because my parents gave me some money for my birthday. Having a stereo was one of those essential things when you moved out of home. I could put up without a lot, but not being able to hear Neil Young was not one of them. (Terry Barlow)

We can hardly leave the subject of music technology without touching upon one of the great icons of the 1970s, the ultimate dream of many teenagers as the coolest and most up-to-date way of playing music at home – the 8 Track Stereo.

Although I only saw a few of them in real life, the 8 Track has stuck in my mind as one of those things that sum up the seventies; men wearing flares, girls in hot pants, the *Generation Game* on the telly and 8 Track stereos, with their bright plastic cases. (K.A. Silverstone)

Some of the most recognisable images from the 1970s span the decade with an eerie precision. Platform shoes are one such thing, which appeared in 1970 and then vanished in 1979, and the 8 Track Stereo is another. The compact tape cassette, which became popular in the 1960s and '70s, suffered from a number of disadvantages as a medium for listening to music; not least of which was the hissing and crackling to which it was prone. In America, a new system was designed, originally meant to be installed in cars – the 8 Track – and it was so successful that home players were also developed. For a while in the early 1970s it was thought that tapes in this format would replace vinyl. Records on vinyl were issued on 8 Track cartridges a month after they appeared as records and the 8 Track looked as though it would sweep all before it.

When I was at university in the mid-seventies, one guy had really rich parents and he had an 8 Track system in his room at college. I can't tell you how cool it made him seem or how popular he became. The thing was based around a bright orange globe, into which the cassettes were pushed. The speakers were made of orange plastic too. The overall effect was to make his room look like something from a science fiction film. His parents had even given him a television for his room as well; an unheard of thing in those days. How we envied that boy! (Geoffrey C. Feldman)

For a time, having an 8 Track Stereo was the pinnacle of 1970s sophistication, making even the most expensive stereo system for records look hopelessly old-fashioned. One version even managed to provide not stereo but quadraphonic sound; four separate channels of music, instead of the two on conventional stereos.

There is not the least doubt that quadraphonic 8 Track sounded fantastic. The sound bounced round the room rather like Dolby stereo today. In fact, even the standard 8 Track was a great improvement on most record players of

the time. Unless you are scrupulously careful, vinyl records
get scratched and dusty, a thing which never happened with
an 8 Track stereo cartridge. Apart from the vastly improved
sound, the thing was so fantastically modern; if you had an
8 Track in 1973, you really were a trend setter. Mind you, if
you still had one ten years later, after the introduction of compact discs, you would have looked a bit sad. (Polly Reynolds)

By 1979, the 8 Track had all but vanished in this country,
outclassed by improvements in the standard audio cassette.
By 1980, it was no longer seen by teenagers as the great-
est music system in the world. It had gone from being the
shape of things to come to being relegated to the scrapheap
of history in just ten short years.

The 8 Track is one of those things that looked so futuristic at
the time and yet aged pretty fast. Today, they look so dated
and old-fashioned that it is hard to believe just what an object
of desire they were for teenagers during the early seventies.
One or two of my friends had them in their bedrooms. One
had been bought an 8 Track for his birthday and the other had
acquired one on hire purchase. They were far more expensive
than ordinary record players and both of the boys I knew who
had them only had two or three cartridges to play. (Anon)

Music of the 1970s

Traditionally, popular music has a very short shelf life. Bill
Haley's 'Rock around the Clock' and Chubby Checker's
'Let's Twist Again', from the 1950s and early 1960s, are
curiosities which enjoyed great popularity in their time; it is
hard to imagine anybody listening to them for pleasure today.

They were attractive to teenagers, but probably to few people over the age of twenty. During the 1970s though, pop music made the transition to mainstream culture. This was part of a general trend, whereby the clothing, hairstyle and tastes of the young came to be adopted by the middle-aged. The case of popular music though was quite astonishing. At the beginning of the 1970s, the majority of parents were still complaining about the supposedly awful racket of the groups that their teenage children were listening to, but by 1980 this sort of music was being heard everywhere. Some were even awarded the ultimate accolade of being turned into muzak for department stores. Teenagers' music had, in effect, become the background soundtrack for the whole of British society.

One thing which I did notice was that at the beginning of the 1970s, there was a sharp division between pop music and the sort of music that my parents listened to. This division blurred as the years passed and by the 1980s they were often listening to the same sort of things as I was. (Chris Arthur)

I suppose that everybody remembers the music that they listened to when they were teenagers and because it evokes fond memories they retain a liking for it, even when they are old and grey. There is probably something of this in the way that today's middle-aged men and women are still fond of seventies music, but there was also the fact that it was simply great! This is of course a subjective judgement, but it cannot be a coincidence that so much of the music from that time is still heard today. You can't say the same for the fifties and sixties. Apart from anything else, there was the sheer variety of the good stuff, which ranged from folk to rock, all the way through to the disco dancing music of the Bee Gees and *Saturday Night Fever*. (Theresa O. Littlestone)

There had been pop music before the 1970s, but this decade's music stands out for the way varying styles dominated the scene before effortlessly spreading and becoming mainstream culture. From Folk singers like Carole King, to rock bands like Black Sabbath and groups like ABBA and the Bee Gees; there really was something for all tastes.

> At risk of sounding like some typical middle-aged man, all the modern pop music sounds the same. It is loud and there is just not the variety that there once was. Just look back to the seventies and think a little about the different hit songs that one might hear; Carly Simon, Slade, Kate Bush, The Who, James Taylor and Crosby Stills. They are all completely different styles of music, with a huge range of types and a lot of experimentation. You can't see anybody still wanting to play any of today's popular music in forty years time, the way that music from the seventies is still played. (Martin O'Connell)

It is a fair guess that if you ask someone who had been a teenager during the 1970s, they will tell you pretty much the same. Music in those days was richer and more melodious, there was a greater variety and it was not so noisy. In fact, recent scientific analysis of popular music over the last half century or so proves that modern music really *is* louder and less varied than that of forty years ago!

In 2012, scientists from the Spanish National Research Council released the results of analysing half a million pop, rock and hip hop tracks from the last fifty years. The results of this work confirmed what middle-aged people are saying today about modern pop music; they reported their findings, stating that, 'We found evidence of a progressive homogenisation of the musical discourse.' They found that recording levels had been increasing steadily over the last five decades – if you played a track from 1970 and another from 2012 at the same volume, the modern one would sound considerably louder.

Their research also revealed that modern popular musicians use a far more restricted range of chords and also a very limited number of chord changes compared with the pop music of the 1970s. They believed that this was due to the fact that modern audiences wanted 'easy' listening; music which was undemanding and intended primarily for relaxation. One of the researchers, Martin Haro of Pompeau Fabra University in Barcelona, said that music from forty or fifty years ago was often concerned with getting a message across, whereas today, young people just want to listen to something which is relaxing.

> I know that the lyrics of some of my favourite bands in the seventies actually mean something. Think about Neil Young's song 'Southern Man' on his album 'After the Gold Rush', which was released in 1970. The whole thing is about racism in the Deep South. Many singers explored contemporary political issues in their music; these songs were designed to challenge listeners and make them think. This is not at all what modern music provides for teenagers today. The majority of the time, all they get now is a strong beat delivered at a high volume. (Terry Barlow)

A Seminal Year for Popular Music

The year 1970 marked a watershed in pop music in various ways. Not only were some very influential albums released in that year, but 1970 also marked the end of several careers in the field of popular music. Most notably, the Beatles broke up in this year. It was also the same year that Jimi Hendrix and Janis Joplin died. Among the albums released in 1970 were 'Deep Purple in Rock' by Deep Purple, 'Bridge Over Troubled Water' by Simon and Garfunkel, 'Black Sabbath' by Black Sabbath, 'Ladies of the Canyon' by Joni Mitchell, 'Atom Heart Mother' by Pink Floyd, 'déjà vu' by Crosby, Stills, Nash and Young, 'After the Gold Rush' by Neil Young, 'Sweet Baby James' by James Taylor, 'Tea for the Tillerman' by Cat Stevens, 'The Tumbleweed Connection' by Elton John, 'Supertramp' and of course the Beatles' last album, 'Let it Be'.

> I don't believe that there has ever been a year for popular music to match 1970. The sheer range of stuff released that year was astonishing. There were gentle ballads like James Taylor singing 'Fire and Rain', as well as heavier music by Black Sabbath and Deep Purple. A lot of this music went on to become the soundtrack to the seventies, defining that time in a very distinctive way. I know that there were popular albums and singers in the 1980s and 1990s, but the seventies seem to have been something special like that and 1970 was the best year of all. (Mick Parker)

Perhaps the most important film in the history of pop music was also released that year. *Woodstock* was a documentary filmed at the Woodstock festival held in America the previous year. It featured songs by The Who, Jimi Hendrix, Janis Joplin, Creedence Clearwater Revival, Grateful Dead, Santana, Melanie and many others. It was released in cinemas at about the same time as another documentary on pop, the Beatles' *Let it Be*, in which they sang tracks from the 'Let it Be' album, which was released earlier that year.

Everybody went to see *Woodstock* at the cinema. It was
said that seeing the film was the next best thing to actually having been there. One slightly irritating thing was
that it was an X, meaning that nobody under the age of
eighteen could see it. This was because of the nudity and
strong language, but it still seems odd that a film about
a music festival should be given the same rating as the
bloodiest horror films. Even today, the DVD carries a
15 rating. (David Ford)

Most popular music from previous decades has faded
away, leaving barely a trace of its passing. However, this
was not at all the case with the sort of music which was
appearing in this particular year, 1970. This was memora-
ble stuff which would continue to sell well for decades into
the future. Well over forty years after the albums in which
they featured were released, there can be few people in
Britain who are not familiar with Simon and Garfunkel's
'Bridge Over Troubled Water' or Paul McCartney's 'The
Long and Winding Road'. This music was not ephemeral,
it was destined to last.

Of course all teenagers feel that the music they enjoy is a
lot better than middle-aged adults can possibly realise.
I am sure that that was the case in the 1940s, '50s and
'60s. There was something about the stuff that was being
produced from 1970s onwards which marked it out. Sure,
there were trashy singles that everybody went mad over and
nobody today has ever heard. But there was also a lot of
music which has lasted and is still well known over forty
years later. The music from that time is still heard all the
time and, what is really interesting, it is still enjoyed by teenagers today. Steve Harley and David Bowie are not merely

historical curiosities but singers who have a substantial following among young people in the twenty-first century. That is odd, because I don't recall any teenagers when I was young in the 1970s being fans of Vera Lynn, for example. Something about the best music of the 1970s has lasted and is still attractive to youngsters now. (Gillian V. McDermott)

As suggested previously, it was the sheer range of exceptionally good music which was released in 1970 which set the tone for the whole decade. Whether you wanted female vocalists singing to an acoustic guitar, like Melanie and Joni Mitchell, or pounding electric guitars, such as those found in Black Sabbath's music, 1970 was the year for buying some incredible albums.

Live Music

In the 1970s, for singers and groups to become established on the British music scene was completely different ballgame from that of today. Recently, we have seen how a group like the Arctic Monkeys have been able to rise to prominence via the internet. Things were very different forty years ago. Not only did bands have to work incredibly hard to be noticed by a record company, but even when they did clinch a deal to cut a disc, their future depended upon favourable reviews and publicity in a small number of magazines, such as *Time Out, Rolling Stone, New Musical Express* and *Melody Maker.* The way to generate sales was to be out on tour in every location, even after you had that all important record deal. This meant that live concerts were much more common in the 1970s, compared to today. In 1971, for example, five years after they had produced their first record for EMI and recorded the sound tracks for several films, including *Zabriskie Point*, Pink Floyd were still performing live in such minor locations as the lecture hall of the University of Essex.

They were glorious times for seeing bands. Big names were appearing in all sorts of out of the way little places and the tickets were always within my means as a student. Some of these events only attracted a few hundred people, but it all helped to spread the word about different groups. I think that the performers used to get a buzz from it, because even after they had made it and were producing albums which were selling well, you would find that they were playing at the Giggleswick Polytechnic or wherever. (K.A. Silverstone)

The London suburb where I lived had several technical colleges within easy reach. Not every week, but often enough, one or other of them would have live music playing. This would vary enormously. One time it was a folk singer called Mike Absalom, then a month later it was a band called Nazareth. No special arrangements were made by the college authorities, they were happy to rent out their place to make a bit of extra cash. Concerts like this were one of the ways of hearing about new music. If a singer couldn't get his records played on the radio, then he had to go round small places and hope that his reputation would spread by word of mouth. The internet has changed all that of course. (Polly Reynolds)

On 1st December 1973, Country Joe McDonald and the All Star Band, who were a massive hit at the 1969 Woodstock Festival, performed at the London School of Economics. Today, this would be inconceivable. Quite apart from any other consideration, health and safety rules would soon put a stop to a rock band playing in the lecture hall of a college.

Nobody stopped to think just how many teenagers you would be able to cram into the lecture hall of a provincial technical college. They just sold as many tickets as they were able and hoped for the best. The toilets were hopelessly inadequate, everybody was smoking, many were drinking and not a few had also, by the look of them, dropped acid. And there, up on the stage of the lecture hall would be one of the biggest names in music, playing our own home town at a price that any penniless student could manage. Country Joe, Pink Floyd, you name them and they probably were playing gigs in out of the way English colleges and universities in the early seventies. (Polly Reynolds)

These was a glorious decade for live music. Without videos or the internet, this was pretty much the only way that teenagers could hope to see their favourite musicians perform. Of course, there were big concerts such as that on the Isle of Wight in 1970, which boasted everybody from Joan Baez and Joni Mitchell to The Doors and The Who. Not all young people could hope to get to these big concerts though and for many it was a matter of waiting for people to play at their local technical college. It is many years since any Further Education College, as they are now known, hosted rock bands or folk singers, but throughout the 1970s these were the places to go to see live music. Local concerts like those at technical colleges were deliberately made affordable. After all, the object of the exercise was partly to publicise the group, and their records were always on sale afterwards.

I was at a technical college in 1971, doing A Levels. We had a few well-known bands perform there, both indoors and out. The prices were always modest and I got the

impression that the aim of the shows was to publicise the
bands as much as to make any money from the actual gig.
For some reason or other, there were singers who were
not much mentioned in the music press but who were
never the less pretty popular. A lot depended on whether
they could get their name in magazines or have their
songs played on the radio. The allegation was at that time
that there was a lot of bribery and corruption and that
musicians had to give backhanders to get themselves pub-
licised in that way. I have no idea how true that was, but I
do know that some bands were well known only because
of the tours which they undertook in small towns across
the country. (Christopher Walker)

Small scale events like those at technical colleges were
very cheap, but many concerts were entirely free. Take
the one in London's Hyde Park on 18th July 1970, for
example. For six hours some of the biggest names in
British music played for an audience of over 120,000
and the entire thing was completely free; Pink Floyd,
Roy Harper, Kevin Ayers, the Edgar Broughton Band –
and all you had to do was make your way there to be
entertained for nothing. Groups like Hawkwind and the
Pink Fairies were regularly playing for free at locations
such as the Westway near Portobello Road.

Summer for many teenagers in the 1970s was a time for
going to festivals and free concerts. In the summer of 1971,
for instance, there was King Crimson playing free at Hyde
Park, and Hawkwind up at Ladbroke Grove. The following
year there was the Windsor Free Festival. Some of the free
music then is fairly hard to believe today. In 1976, Queen
played to an audience of over two hundred thousand at

Hyde Park; again, absolutely free. We used to arrive at these
places on the night before, like shoppers in the sales, staking
out a good position near the stage. (Christopher Walker)

Attending concerts and festivals of this sort became an
annual ritual for many teenagers. They would hitchhike
to the venue and the weekend would cost next to nothing. It is hard to grasp now just how accessible live music
was at that time, the most famous names in pop music
playing either for nothing or at prices that any teenager
could afford. It made commercial sense for the artists, as
these events were brilliant publicity and after having seen
the group live the majority of fans would buy their album.
Reading about concerts in *Time Out* or *Melody Maker*,
discussing them with friends, travelling to the venue,
crashing in the open air; all this made the following of a
band an absorbing hobby for many teenagers.

In the 1990s, my daughter would go to concerts featuring
her favourite bands. These events were always tightly con-
trolled and the prices astronomical. The numbers attending
were strictly limited, security guards were present and there
was of course no question of smoking or taking in a few
cans of beer. She found it incredible to think that I had seen
people like Queen and Pink Floyd for free in the 1970s. It
was another world. (Polly Reynolds)

2

Communications

In the 1970s, the art of writing letters to lovers and friends was slowly coming to an end. This was a by-product of the technological advances being made in all fields, but particularly in telecommunications. Apart from exchanging letters, almost all friendships and any other relationships were carried on face-to-face, rather than being mediated by electronic media as is the case today. But how did people get together in the first place in those far off days when there was no form of social media.

Trying to track somebody down could be pretty hard. When I was at college in 1973 most of the people I knew weren't on the phone and so it was a matter of actually going round and knocking on people's doors. If you wanted to arrange to go to a concert or something, you would usually have to speak face-to-face with all the people involved. Sometimes, for a large event, we would put up a card or poster in the college, but apart from that, communication was very much one-to-one. If there was a party, you could ask one person to tell somebody else, but the only reliable method was to hunt down the person and speak to them. (Esther M. Hannigan)

On the face of it, teenagers are far more connected and able to communicate with each other than when I was a teenager myself in the late seventies. They can chat on mobiles, gossip on Instant Messenger, look at Facebook, text and email each other from their bedrooms to anywhere in the world. What is missing though is often the face-to-face social life that we had when I was young. At that time, nearly every contact I had with any friend was when the two of us were in close physical proximity; in a room together or on a bus, say. Some of the conversations were by telephone, of course, and a very few were by means of the printed word. The proportions have now almost precisely been reversed. Today, the great majority of contact that teenagers have with each other is by the printed word, via texts, Facebook and so on. Even when they are with each other, they are still communicating with other by printed word. It is common to see groups of teenagers walking along the street and texting as they go. They are with their friends, but their communication is really with others by tapping out messages on a keyboard. (Gillian V. Pettitt)

A college noticeboard was one method of finding out what sort of things were going on in the area, which might be of interest to you and your friends. To keep in touch, the eighteen and nineteen year olds attending lectures would check this wall regularly. Other young people would also come to the college to find out what was going on in their particular circle. True, there were magazines like *Time Out* with listings of events for the coming week, but noticeboards would be specifically geared to a few square miles of one suburb or district of a town or city. You could even pin up personal messages, perhaps asking Mary Brown to ring you on a certain number. These places were the forerunner of the Facebook 'wall'; a genuine wall covered in messages and information.

I don't think that teenagers today realise how much effort one had to put into keeping in touch with what was happening. You had to read magazines like *Time Out*, *IT*, *Oz* and *Melody Maker*, as well as checking out the notice-board in the local technical college. You would also need to ring friends and find out if they had heard of anything happening that weekend. Some events, such as the first ever gay march in London, which took place in 1971, spread almost entirely by word of mouth. These days, of course, you just Google a few key words and you will find out about pretty much anything happening anywhere in the world. (Christopher Walker)

It makes me laugh when my daughter talks about her 'wall' on Facebook. When I tell her that as a teenager I was dependent upon a physical wall to keep in touch with what was happening among friends and fellow students, she looks at me as though I am mad. Students in the seventies did not often have telephones, other than possibly a communal payphone in the hallway of a house split up into bedsits. We used to write messages for people and leave them where they would see them. Things like, 'Kath, we are meeting at the George tonight at seven'. Things were passed by word of mouth, but then it became a game of Chinese Whispers, with the message becoming more and more distorted as it made the rounds. (Sarah P. Moran)

Are You on the Telephone?

The majority of British households throughout the whole of the 1970s did not have telephones. Incredibly, it was only as late as 1982 that the percentage of homes in this country with telephones reached 50 per cent. Today, every member of a family is likely to be on the telephone with his or her separate mobile phone; a state of affairs which would have seemed like something out of a science fiction film to teenagers in the 1970s.

My parents weren't on the phone and it made life very difficult for me. I could ring people from call boxes, but nobody could get in touch with me. I used to think that this had the effect of making me appear a little desperate. Other people could wait for people to ring them, but if I'd done that, I would never have seen anybody. (Theresa O. Littlestone)

When you met someone who was not on the phone, you had to get their address so that you could write to them. We were on the phone and if I wanted to get to know somebody who wasn't, say someone I had met at a party, I would ask for their address. Then I could write to the girl, as it usually was, and ask her to ring me. She would do this from a phone box and we could then make arrangements to get together. It wasn't really the thing in those first stages of a friendship or relationship just to turn up on the doorstep unannounced and so you had to find ways to fix things up. Letters and call boxes did the trick. (Geoffrey C. Feldman)

Not only were telephones not universal at that time, but telephone bills were comparatively expensive. One did not spend hours on the phone chatting to friends. Needless to say there were no mobiles, but the ordinary landline was almost invariable placed in the hallway; the most public part of the average home. Anything approaching an intimate or even vaguely private conversation was quite out of the question and standing in a draughty hallway by the front door did not make one feel exactly relaxed. Telephone calls were functional things in those days, not something to be undertaken willy-nilly for no other purpose than to gossip to a schoolmate.

You see kids chatting all the time on their mobiles now. I was fourteen in 1972, and although we had a telephone it was not used for lengthy conversations. It was in the hall and if I rang one of my friends, my father was sure to walk past after a few minutes, going through a pantomime ritual of looking at his watch and gesturing at me to speed it up. For his generation, making a telephone call was something you did for a purpose; not just because you felt like a chat. If it was an important call, I would go to a call box, but then there was often a queue there and people glaring at you reproachfully if you took too long. It was usually easier just to go round people's houses if you wanted to talk. (Terry Barlow)

The telephone in the hall! Great for those delicate moments when your girlfriend has just told you that she loves you and wants to know why you will not say the same thing to her. The fact that your mum is in the kitchen, well within earshot and your younger sister is passing through the hall would have a lot to do with that. Even worse were the times when you were in the throes of breaking up and all the recriminations and abject apologies had to be played out to an audience consisting of whichever family members happened to be around at the time. (Paul Clarke)

To hold a completely private conversation usually entailed going to that person's house, or vice versa. These days, teenagers can immediately establish – via Facebook, Twitter, skype or text – the precise location of any friend whom they wish to see. When the majority of one's friends did not even have a telephone at home, there was nothing for it but to go searching for the person one wanted to see. This was not really regarded as a nuisance; it was part of the fun. One would head off to see Jim or Joe and perhaps meet Jack on the way. He would mention that Joe had been seen round John's house and so a change of direction was made towards John's.

Meeting up with friends and seeing people was an end in itself. Catching up with a particular person was not at all straightforward, but that was part of the whole scene: walking round to X's house and then hearing from his mum that he was out with Y. There were certain places where our bunch often hung out, such as the café in the local park. If you wanted to find somebody, you could always go there and see if anybody had seen the person. If you didn't find the person you had set out to find, then at least you would be sure of bumping into somebody else. I don't believe that my own children ever have this experience. Every meeting which they have is constantly updated by text and telephone conversation, they always know within a few yards where they can find any particular person. (Gillian V. Pettitt)

My father collared every boy I went out with when he came to call for me. I would be up in my room getting ready and come down the stairs to find that my new boyfriend had already arrived and my father was asking him what he did for a living, what school he had been to and a hundred other things. In those days, it was considered polite to call for a girl rather than just meeting her somewhere. I used to dread it when I made a new friend, because my parents always found out all about them and were free in passing on their opinions of the person to me later. My own daughter has all sorts of friends I have never met. They ring her on her mobile to let her know that they are outside and so most of the time I never even get a chance to say hello to them. (Polly Reynolds)

The methods of communications used in the seventies meant a lot less privacy for teenagers. Letters could be scrutinised. If one had just been on holiday to Spain and then letters with Spanish stamps started landing on the doormat, it was bound to invite questions. Similarly, if somebody rang for me, my parents would always ask, 'Who's speaking, please?' This enabled one's parents to build up some sort of picture of who you were associating with. Today, the children make all their arrangements through email, text and skype. It is far harder for their parents to keep track of what is going on. (Theresa O. Littlestone)

The haphazard and random wandering around in search of friends allowed evenings and weekends to develop in a far more fluid way than is now the case. A Saturday morning which started with a vague plan of going round to see Mary could change as a result of meeting Tom on the way there and you could end up going into town with him instead. Mary would never even know that you had been heading towards her home and the entire day would turn out very differently from expected.

A lot of the time when I was young seemed to be spent looking for people – I would go out on Saturday afternoon, hoping to bump into people in town. There were a few places where we used to hang round; a café, certain shops, the park in summer. You could generally be sure of finding somebody if you wandered about those places. Once you had seen one person, they might tell you that somebody else had been heading towards some pub or other and so you could walk there. There was very often no sort of plan to the day; it would just develop according to who you met and what they were doing. I suppose that things would have been very different if we could actually have spoken to all our friends or exchanged text messages, the way teenagers today do. They can always locate anybody they want at once. (Gillian V. Pettitt)

A lot of teenagers today plan their evenings like a military operation. They are texting every two minutes to check where every member of their group is at any given moment. There is little chance of any random changes in their arrangements. To my mind, this must take a lot of the fun out of things. In our town there were one or two pubs where you could always go to pick up with people you knew. Half of them weren't on the phone anyway and so you could not really fix things up in advance. But if we turned up at one of those pubs, we knew that we would bump into people. I would have hated to have all the people I knew in those days to be able to get in touch with me at any moment. Obviously, there were times when you wanted to slip out and avoid people. (Paul Clarke)

If you had arranged to meet your friends in the pub and the bus broke down, you could arrive to find that they had moved on to another and wholly unknown destination. All this added an unpredictable element to many evenings. It also resulted in making new friends; conversations might start with strangers as a result of trying to find out whether your friends had been at a certain place earlier that day. Life for teenagers without telephones was certainly more haphazard.

> Hardly any of the people that I was seeing in the mid-seventies were on the phone. You could try knocking on their door, but often you would find it easier simply to go to their haunts. The Lyons in the High Road was a place where everybody seemed to go on Saturdays and if you sat there long enough over a cup of coffee, almost everybody you knew would pass through. If I hadn't made any special arrangement on a Saturday, I would sometimes pop into Lyons café and just wait until somebody I knew came in.

Instant communication with everybody one knows might seem to be an unalloyed good, but it has certainly destroyed the way of life known to teenagers in previous generations. Though this might not necessarily be a bad thing, it is undeniable that it has happened. Of course, the invention of telephones, radio and the telegraph also had profound effects on the way in which young people in this country conducted their lives. The changes that we have seen over the last three or four decades, though, seem to have been more wide reaching than those which accompanied the arrival of previous advances in the technology of communication.

> In about 1975 or 1976, we had a phone installed at my parents' house. By the end of that summer, my whole way of life had changed. People could contact me more easily and I fell into the habit of making arrangements before I went out, instead of just seeing how the day developed. It was far more convenient, but there is no doubt that my life as a seventeen-year-old

changed radically from how it had been before. Much of that was due to 'being on the phone'. (Terry Barlow)

Young people are naturally 'early adopters' of new technology and so it is their lives which have been most affected in recent years by such things as instant messaging, texts and social networking sites. The result is that for many teenagers today, the way of life known to their parents and grandparents is utterly incomprehensible.

Public Call Boxes

During the 1970s, one of the only ways that any teenager could have a private telephone conversation was by using a public telephone. Picture the scene. You want to remind your girlfriend how much you love her, but you certainly don't want to make such a statement where your mother might walk past at any moment! The solution was to go out to a call box and ring her from there. Of course, she would be guarded in her responses because she would not be afforded the same privacy – the exact reason you were using a phone box. You could tell her that you loved her passionately and her answer would be limited perhaps to 'Me too'.

I cannot remember when last I used a public telephone. They used to be a big part of my life as a teenager. We weren't on the phone and so I had to go out to ring people up. In those days they had telephone directories in them. There was often a queue and there was an intricate code of etiquette associated with the process. Sometimes, if it was urgent, you could ask if you could nip in front of somebody and make your call first. Being a girl, I found that this often worked with men. You have to remember too that many of those calls were being made by adults to the council or electricity board or something important like that. It wasn't just teenagers using call boxes and it was definitely considered bad form to gossip for hours if other people were waiting to use the phone. (Sarah P. Moran)

Most of the telephone conversations that I remember from the seventies took place in phone boxes. So much so that I can still mentally reconstruct the interior of call boxes at that time. There was a shelf for putting your bag on and also telephone directories on swivels, so that you could look up numbers. You did not put your money in the slot until the pips started going when the other person answered. Actually, you could use call boxes for sending messages for free. I had one girlfriend whose father couldn't stand me and who did not like me ringing his daughter. We had an arrangement whereby I would ring her house and let the phone ring twice and then hang up. If I did this twice, it meant that I was would be waiting for her round the corner from her house. She would give it a few minutes after the phone had rung so that it didn't look fishy and then beetle out on the pretext of going to the shops. (Christopher Walker)

For relationships hindered by distance, for example holiday romances or one of the couple moving to the other side of the country for university, call boxes sometimes came in handy. Relationships of this kind could be nurtured to some extent by letters, but they both benefited from the occasional telephone conversation to keep them alive. Since students didn't have their own telephones, they had to ring their paramours from a call box from time to time to reassure them that they had not been forgotten, and that even though they were separated by distance their love was

as strong as ever and they were counting the days until the
end of term. Unfortunately, the average life of relationships
of this kind would be around two months.

> I was sixteen when my eighteen-year-old boyfriend went off
> to Exeter to study history in 1974. We swore eternal love
> and he promised to ring every Saturday from a payphone.
> This worked fine for the first six weeks or so and then one
> Saturday he didn't ring. I got a letter the next week telling
> me it was over. I have sometimes wondered if things would
> have been different if we could have spoken every day,
> instead of just once a week. (Theresa O. Littlestone)

> My girlfriend didn't live that far away, only the other side of
> the Thames, but during the week I could only speak to her
> by using a phone box. Her parents were on the phone and
> mine weren't. It meant going out to ring her in the even-
> ing. Often there would be people waiting to use the phone
> and I felt guilty about chatting to her for long. Sometimes
> she wasn't in and that would mean going home and then
> trying again later. Then again, I might come out and forget
> to bring a supply of 2p and 5p coins. It was a right hassle
> and did not always put me in the right frame of mind for a
> romantic conversation. (Mick Parker)

Holiday romances were often between people from a different class or background. Statistically, the odds of both
parties having a telephone at home were slim and so here
again the public call box came into play. As with the long-
distance university romance, such affairs tended not to last.

> In 1975, when I was nineteen, I had a girlfriend in France.
> Although neither of our families were on the phone, we still

found a way to talk every day. We fixed up by letter that I
would be in a certain phone box at a set time and send her
the number of the box. Then she would ring the operator
from another call box and ask to make a reverse charge call. I
answered the phone and accepted the call and we could chat
for as long as we wanted. I suppose it was illegal, but it worked
very well and we never got caught. (Christopher Walker)

Call boxes were very popular with teenagers at this time,
although it could be quite difficult to find one which was not
in use and it was not at all uncommon to have queues of
young people waiting to use a box. Sometimes the conversations would be lengthy and emotional and it was clear that
love affairs were being conducted by the youngster in the red
box. Of course, this could be irritating if one just wished to
make a quick call. However, there was a certain amount of
leeway given to young lovers, and a teenager carrying on a a a
passionate love affair when there was a long queue of people
waiting to use the phone would be judged less harshly than a
middle-aged man arguing with the gas board.

A girl I was going out with was due to move to Ireland with
her family in 1974. I was cut up about it and was trying
to persuade her to stay in England and get a flat with me
instead. She was only eighteen and it was too much to ask of
her. Because my parents weren't on the phone, I had to beg
and plead with her from a call box and as you can imagine,
these calls were long and intricate. Those waiting to use the
box were very patient and on one occasion, after I had been
raising my voice in supplication, I suddenly realised that
everybody in the queue could hear me. When I left, nobody
looked annoyed and one old woman said, 'Never mind,
love, there's plenty more fish in the sea.' (K.A. Silverstone)

As the decade drew on, more and more homes acquired telephones. On 25th September 1976, the girls' magazine *Jackie* carried an article about telephones, and it claimed that, 'Dial phones could soon be a thing of the past. Fast push-button phones are now being installed in places all over the country. You simply press a button for each number you want.' The first such domestic telephones appeared in the 1970s. The Trimphone, a clunky British version of the new phones, looks as dated today as an old candlestick phone from the 1920s!

Letters

By far the most common way for teenagers to keep in touch was by letters. If neither party had a telephone at home, they had no other choice but to write to one another. Of course, these were the days when the post was delivered twice a day and the first post generally came about eight o'clock in the morning. Some people today may turn their nose up at teenagers ending relationships by text. In the 1970s, however, breaking up with somebody with whom a holiday romance had been conducted was simplicity itself if the relationship was being carried out by letter; you simply stopped writing, with no explanation at all! Without telephones and with the other person living a couple of hundred miles away, this was a foolproof method of ending a friendship with no embarrassment.

> When I was fifteen we went on holiday to Butlin's at Skegness. This was in 1972. I fell in love with a young man who worked there and we spent a lot of time together, although it didn't amount to any more than kissing and cuddling. When we went home to Birmingham, we exchanged

addresses and wrote frequently at first. Unusually for this kind of romance, it was me who lost interest first and I just sort of let my letters dry up. He got increasingly desperate; I think that perhaps he really was in love with me. Fortunately, he didn't fulfil his threat of turning up on my doorstep! (Theresa O. Littlestone)

A purely psychological thing, but I was far less glib and apt to tell a lie when I was writing letters to the person with whom I was in love than I would be sending an email. I know it's irrational, but I used to agonise while composing letters to my boyfriend. It was important to me to analyse my feelings and do my best to be honest. I suppose that putting things down in permanent form like that had something to do with it. These days we type things on our computers everyday, but forty years ago, writing a letter was a rarer event. It wasn't like having an ordinary conversation; the letters you wrote meant something. I wouldn't have liked to send something which was not as truthful as I could manage to make it. (Polly Reynolds)

I still have letters that my boyfriend sent me in 1977, when we were eighteen. He was a right one, very popular and a bit of a show-off, but in his letters he was struggling to be honest about his feelings. He couldn't be serious when we were together or even when we were talking on the phone, but in his letters, a more sensitive person could be seen. (Theresa O. Littlestone)

The pace of the relationship was moderated and slowed by the rhythm of sending a letter and then waiting for a reply. Both sides had time to take stock and mull over in their minds what was going on and how they wanted things to progress in the future. Teenagers sending letters to each other were able to savour their feelings; the mechanism of love letters becomes a fulfilling activity in itself.

> My girlfriend and I only lived a mile or so from each other and yet we still wrote each other letters regularly. If we had had a row or something, then it was common for one of us to write to the other, explaining things from our side. This gave us a chance to sit down and think the thing over without any pressure. I still have some of those letters. Sitting down in your bedroom and struggling to put your deepest feelings into a proper letter helps put things into perspective. The last of those letters was dated September 1977, when we were eighteen. I wonder if any teenager today will be treasuring sheets of paper with writing on them done in fountain pen. (Terry Barlow)

> I don't believe that teenagers send letters to each other any more. Why would they want to? They can just tap in the words on a mobile and someone can read them in a second or two. There is something about writing a letter and putting it into an envelope and then going out to post it which is qualitatively different from sending an email or text. For one thing, this is a personal communication, one which is unlikely to be read by anybody other than the intended recipient. An awful lot of communications which teenagers now make to each other are public property and that puts them into another category entirely. Send a letter to a friend and it is extremely unlikely that anybody else will even see the thing. Perhaps one or two others might glimpse it, but it can never become common property. This is in contrast to a message on a Facebook wall or even an email or text. Teenagers show each other texts that they have received all the time and emails also get forwarded to others. This awareness, that other people might read what you are

writing, makes a teenager's email to somebody quite different from a personal letter. (Anon)

Letters between teenagers sometimes contained photographs. Here again is a very great difference in the world of forty years ago. Now, one can snap a picture on a mobile phone and email it to anybody in the world in a fraction of a second. The only way of transmitting a photograph anywhere in the 1970s was by sending it in the post. Teenagers' photographs were generally one of two types. The first sort was black and white photo booth pictures. Often, more than one person was seen in such pictures and they were, as a rule, sticking out their tongues or pulling silly faces.

I have seen pictures of teenagers from their Facebook page, all of which seem to be of their friends sticking out their tongues, making faces and generally looking silly. I have to confess that I have made disparaging remarks about these. After all, what's the point? While clearing out an old drawer recently, I came across some strips of black and white pictures from a photo booth. They show me and three friends, all crammed into the booth to make sure that our pictures were taken together. All of us are gurning away furiously. The date is scribbled on the back; 26th August 1976. (Sarah P. Moran)

The first time I went out with the girl I eventually married, at my suggestion we popped into a photo booth on the way home. It was October 1973 and she was just sixteen. I cut the strip of four black and white photos in half and we had two each. I know that these days everybody has cameras on their phones, but at that time being photographed was not nearly as common. Those black and white pictures are the only images I have of myself for that year. (David Ford)

The other kind of photographs were blurry, under-exposed, over-exposed or out of focus colour pictures taken with an Instamatic camera. Cameras like the Kodak Instamatic were popular with young people. They were relatively cheap and loading the film meant just dropping a plastic cassette in, rather than threading a spool, which one had to do with 35mm cameras. There were no controls to worry about either; you just pointed the thing and clicked the shutter.

> The only camera I remember any of my friends having was the old Instamatic. It was easy to use, no controls to set or anything. You just pointed it and clicked the shutter. The pictures were often blurred and they seemed to fade after a time. Looking at some of those old colour snapshots now, they looked as dated as anything. For one thing, the pictures they took were square. All my old photographs from the seventies are square. Just ask yourself when the last time you saw a square photograph was? It was almost certainly taken with an Instamatic. My teenage life was recorded from 1973 to 1980 in square photographs with white borders. As soon as you see them, you know at once that they are from thirty or forty years ago. The colour has bleached out from them and every youth in them is wearing flares or bell-bottom jeans. (Paul Clarke)

Square photographs taken with an Instamatic are by way of being some of the most common mementos from this era – the faded image of some long-haired youth wearing bell-bottoms; the group of teenagers smiling at the camera with a pop concert in the background; the last day at school. Those old square photos are symbolic of teenage life in the 1970s, the only remaining visual images for many of their youth in those days.

> I still have a photograph of the first girl I ever truly loved. She and her family emigrated to Australia in 1975, when I was nineteen. It is a square picture with a white border around it and looks incredibly old-fashioned. Taken with my Instamatic, it shows Janice smiling sadly at me in the back garden of my parent's house, the day before she flew out of my life forever. She took one of me at the same time and I sometimes wonder whether she sometimes gazes at that, as I do at the one of her, wondering about those teenagers almost forty years ago. (Christopher Walker)

> I couldn't afford to take all that many photographs when I was a teenager. Developing the film was expensive and so I would usually only buy a film for some special event. This meant that the photographs taken when I was young, say from 1975 to the early 1980s, have a jerky and discontinuous feel. You didn't just keep a film in your camera and take pictures from time to time, you would buy a film for a holiday or because you were going out for the day. (Sarah P. Moran)

In an age where photographs are taken a hundred times a day, with most people having cameras on their mobile phones better than most models from the 1970s, it can be hard to remember that taking photographs was once a chancy and uncertain enterprise. One never knew how they would turn out until you got them back from the chemist. Photography was an expensive hobby, one which could only really be indulged on special occasions; holidays, Christmas, weddings and other notable events.

In the seventies, you would only buy a film for the camera
on special occasions. You might get one if you were going
on holiday, for instance, or for leaving school or at a wedding. The pictures which I have from the late seventies
are like that, with six-month gaps between them. Here I
am on the last day of school in July 1977, then there is a
Christmas party that year, followed by a summer holiday in
1978. (K.A. Silverstone)

The Kodak Instamatic, which was the most commonly
used cheap camera of the time, was essentially no more
than a box camera, with fixed focus and exposure. It really
needed to be used in bright sunshine for the pictures to be
clear and bright. Unless lighting and the distance of the
subject from the camera were completely right, the results
could be pretty awful; as many snapshots from this sort
of camera testify. Since these pictures were physically
irreplaceable, they were very precious. They could not be
electronically duplicated, and in most cases no more than a
single copy ever existed.

I used to be quite keen on taking photographs when I was
at university. I say quite keen; I mean that I might have used
up a roll of film a term. Although I was quite a dedicated
photographer in this way from 1972-75 when I was up at
Warwick, I have today only half a dozen or so photographs
from those days. There are several reasons for this. First,
of course, you might shoot off an entire roll of film and
then find that half of them were blurred or hopelessly
under-exposed. Then friends would beg for copies of any
of the pictures which showed them. I knew that I could
order extra copies from the chemist, but that was one of
the things which one never quite got round to doing. The

negatives became lost over the years, as did some of the pictures, which leaves me with just six or seven square photographs to remember those days by. (Christopher Walker)

The colours faded in these photographs, leaving a bleached-out look, no matter how perfect the conditions were at the time they were taken. These pictorial records of teenage life in the 1970s are as distinctive as sepia-tinted Victorian daguerreotype images.

Everything about the photographs which I still have from the seventies looks positively ancient. We are so used today to high definition: bright, lifelike colour and razor-sharp focus that it rather jumps out at us when these things are missing. Some of the photographs I still have from when I was at college in 1970-72 are in black and white. In the later, colour ones, time has robbed the colours of the vibrancy, leaving them looking a little sepia tinted. The young people in the pictures all have a posed air about them as well. They are standing upright and smiling self-consciously. (Polly Reynolds)

We all look as stiff as dummies in the window of a clothing shop in the photographs of me and my friends when we were leaving school. Perhaps it was because we were less used to being photographed then. My father only took one reel of film a year, and because it was expensive we were all commanded to stand stock still and smile. There is that same artificial and posed quality to the shots of me in school uniform in the summer of 1972, a few days before I left. (K.A. Silverstone)

The chief difference about the mementos and records of teenage lives from the 1970s is that letters, documents and photographs were almost invariably one-offs; they were irreplaceable. If you lost that photograph of you at Christmas in 1974 it was gone forever, and there were only single copies of any letter. All this has changed now, however, and emails sent to a teenager may be copied endlessly, forwarded to anybody else and so linger on in the inboxes of other recipients, even if deleted by the person who first received it. The same is true of photographs. They are saved onto memory cards, copied onto laptop hard drives and posted on half a dozen sites across the internet. Instead of one copy, there may be dozens taken by chance with a seventeen year olds' mobile phone.

> I am constantly astounded at how many people seem to have knowledge about the most trivial of my son's activities. He is nineteen and if he visits a town with a friend, he will tweet about it, take pictures and send them to friends, write about the trip on Tumblr, put pictures up on his Facebook page. It almost seems like immortality of a sort; that the record of that outing is scattered permanently in a dozen places. When I was his age, all I would have from such a casual afternoon would be memories. (Gillian V. Pettitt)

It remains to be seen how permanent the pictures taken and the words typed into mobiles and laptops will actually be. If it is easy to take photographs and type messages in this way, it is just as easy to delete them at the click of a button. The old letters and photographs treasured by today's fifty and sixty year olds may have a fleeting and ephemeral feel to them, but it is possible that they may outlast the hundreds of snapshots and emails being created and exchanged by teenagers today.

3

Fashion

The overall impression that many people have of the 1970s is that it was a time of atrocious fashions and colourful décor; an era when people apparently took leave of their senses, at least as far as personal appearance was concerned. Looking at photographs of what people were wearing in the decades either side of the 1970s reveals some strange ideas of what is attractive in clothes and hairstyles, but the 1970s remain in a class of their own. This was a very significant time though for fashion and the effects of changing tastes from this decade affect us all, even today. Since, as is usually the case, teenagers were at the cutting edge of the prevailing style of that time, it might be worth looking at the influences at work.

I missed being a teenager in the seventies by seven or eight years. When I left school in the early sixties, there was no question of dressing in anything other than a conservative way. I wanted to work in an office and it would have been unthinkable for me to wear anything other than a collar and tie and have my hair ruthlessly cut every month.

Because I didn't earn that much, I used to wear much the same clothes at the weekend as I wore for work. It never really occurred to me to do otherwise. During the seventies, I started to see young men in their late teens dressing in what would have been outrageous fashions only ten years earlier. Their hair was flopping down all over the place and they didn't bother with ties when going out. Girls sometimes wore make-up and at other times didn't bother and many let their hair grow naturally, without doing anything with it. I began to feel that I had been born ten years too early. What was curious was that these new styles and more informal way of dressing were now becoming to be accepted even in formal settings. It wasn't just pop singers and beatniks who were allowing their hair to grow, it was happening everywhere. It may have started with teenagers, but older men were keen to let their hair down and become more relaxed and informal in how they dressed and kept their hair. This is a trend which has lasted and can still be seen today. (Anon)

Before the 1970s, men of all ages, from schoolboys to pensioners, had very short hair. Facial hair was uncommon and unless you were either in the navy or were a popular television eccentric, was likely to be limited to a small moustache. Even these were not common in the decade immediately preceding the 1970s. Any other sort of peculiarity in the hair line, such as sideboards or hair over the collar, was definitely the preserve of pop stars or artists. For teenage girls, the convention was that hair remained long until you were at least in your twenties.

I remember my mother despairing of me because I left my hair alone and just let it grow and do what it wanted. For her, this was a really slovenly way for a girl to approach life. Respectable girls who cared about themselves spent hours each week fussing about their hair and put on make-up every morning before they left the house. I found it so liberating in the seventies to wash my hair and let it dry naturally, or go for a week without putting on any make-up. For women of my mother's generation though, there was something slightly scandalous about a seventeen-year-old girl being so careless about her appearance. She really didn't get it and would talk of the need for me to, 'Make more of myself' and not to 'Let myself go'. It was almost as though it was a moral issue, rather than just a change in fashion. (Pat Howard)

When I stopped having my hair cut regularly, my father began to get restless. I wasn't letting it grow long, I wasn't putting it in a ponytail or anything, but it still made him uneasy. This would have been around 1971, when I was sixteen or seventeen. By modern standards it was still pretty short, just peeping over the collar, but it was very important to my father. Having hair that wasn't shaved right up the back of the neck each month made one look at best scruffy and at worst like a drug addict or student. Of course, at that age there is often friction over one thing or another and the more he went on about it, the longer I would leave it between going to the barber. (Christopher Walker)

Clothing for teenagers in the years leading up to the 1970s was, except for various groups like beatniks, hippies, mods or bikers, pretty much the same as their parents' clothing. They could flout the conventions to some degree, but the basic style of accepted and 'respectable' clothing and appearance, especially for men, remained largely unchanged from the end of the First World War until the start of the 1970s. This can be summed up as short hair for men, with collars and ties for all formal occasions and a lot of leisure activities, and skirts and dresses for women, with a great deal of attention paid to their hair and other aspects of their appearance.

> One of the things that really wound up older people during the late sixties and early seventies was the trend for teenage girls and boys to dress similarly. Not all of them, obviously, but it happened enough to become the sort of thing that cartoonists would poke fun at and comedians would crack jokes about. Boys' hair was getting longer and girls were wearing jeans a lot and there was unisex clothing about. The result was that a boy and his girlfriend might both wear jeans, have their hair the same length and also have on similar types of jumpers or T-shirts. 'Can't tell if it's a boy or a girl,' became something of a catchphrase for the older generation. This is referenced in the David Bowie song from the 1974 album, 'Diamond Dogs': 'You've got your mother in a whirl, she can't tell if you're a boy or a girl'. I could never understand what it was about this that used to drive older men in particular mad. They used to get so angry about the whole business. (Geoffrey C. Feldman)

> My son and daughter both wore much the same clothes when they were teenagers in the nineties. She had shortish hair and his was longish and both lived in blue jeans. My parents were always going on about their supposed inability to distinguish the male singers from the females when they watched *Top of the Pops*. It was almost an obsession when I was a teenager myself and they were not the only ones. It was really important to them to be able to tell at

a glance whether they were looking at a boy or girl. There really were occasions when my kids were fourteen or so, when I honestly did not know which of them was coming down the street. What baffles me is why anybody would get worked up about this. (Maria T. Valentine)

For centuries it had been thought outrageous for women to wear trousers instead of skirts. From time to time it would be done, but the fashion was never widely adopted. Then, entirely as a result of what teenagers were choosing to wear, this steadfast clothing code withered away. Many women wear trousers and jeans nowadays and nobody bats an eyelid. A sartorial division which had lasted for over a thousand years in this country fell by the wayside as teenage fashions conquered all ages.

I can still remember when girls wearing jeans were regarded as being a little daring. At the very least, it made one look a bit of a rebel. This was in the early sixties. Then it was no longer just a handful of young women, almost every teenage girl suddenly seemed to have a pair of jeans. From there, it spread to older women. At first, older women would only wear trouser suits, but then they too took to jeans. Now, of course, jeans are the uniform of the teenager and also worn by all ages and both sexes. It was teenagers in the seventies who triggered this revolution. (Nina Webb)

What had started as trends by minor youth subcultures during the 1960s had spread by the early 1970s to many young people. Somewhere during the course of the decade, these fashion trends made the transition from teenagers to the general population. By 1980, it was common to see men of all ages with their hair over their collars or even with ponytails. Women were wearing trousers for even the most formal events and they were even allowed in the Royal Enclosure at Ascot. Ties began to be abandoned at weekends and shirts left open to expose the chest. Again, this began with teenagers and then quickly spread. The so-called 'medallion man' became a stock figure of the 1970s; the grown man with no tie and his shirt open to expose his chest, often adorned with a gold medallion or other piece of jewellery. This too was a radical departure from tradition. For over a century, it had been generally agreed that any man wearing a piece of jewellery other than just a signet ring was sure to be a homosexual. Now jewellery for men became all the rage.

> My father disapproved very strongly of any sort of jewellery worn by men; 'Makes him look like a pansy boy,' was his invariable judgement on any identity bracelet, medallion, beads, anything, in fact, other than a signet ring. This was not some quirk of my father's; it was a widespread feeling that there was something effeminate about a man wearing jewellery. This changed over the course of the seventies. By the time that the eighties arrived it was fine for men to wear gold chains, bracelets and various other things. The man with a hairy chest and a gold medallion became something of an image for the times. (Martin O'Connell)

So far, we have looked at teenage styles which crossed over into the mainstream. The influence of these is seen today in both men and women's fashion. There were also, of course, fashions in teenage clothing which did not last and have faded away. Take hot pants for example. Hot pants were really no more than very short shorts worn by young women. Women had worn shorts before the 1970s, of course, but chiefly on the beach or when hiking. Hot pants, though, were very brief and the whole point was that they were intended to be fashionable clothes to be worn on any occasion. Hot pants first made their appearance in the late 1960s, but by 1970 they were being worn by many teenage girls. Previously, shorts for women had been very clearly intended for casual wear, but the hot pants on sale in boutiques in the early 1970s were in various materials and styles, some of which were supposed to be suitable for formal wear.

> I badgered my mother into buying me a pair of hot pants when I was fourteen, in 1971. They were very smart, grey with a bib front. She didn't quite realise what she was doing, I think, because I think that she had some vague idea that I would only be wearing the things when I was playing in the park or something! When my father saw me in them for the first time he hit the roof. They were very short, almost up to my crotch, and I suppose that showing that much leg was a bit much for a girl of fourteen. There was endless haggling and negotiation about the circum-stances and places that I was allowed to wear them and they caused more trouble than they were worth in the end. I think that apart from being taken aback by how short they were, he was genuinely afraid that I would be inviting trouble from men. (Theresa O. Littlestone)

In more recent times, teenagers are once again wearing 'hot pants', although they are now known more widely as just shorts. The desire to expose as much bare flesh as possible started in the late 1960s, with the invention of the miniskirt – hot pants were really an extension of this idea. A taboo on women's underwear being visible, which restricted the length – or lack of length – of the miniskirt, was not such an issue with hot pants; they could have quite decently been worn without any underwear at all!

The crop top, another fashion of the decade, also allowed as much skin to be shown as possible. These were tops which revealed the belly and often the shoulders too. The combination of hot pants and crop tops, which one saw on the streets in the early 1970s, was akin to a bikini. Those older people who complained about the androgynous look of many teenagers could hardly have cause to protest about this look; there was little doubt about the gender of a teenage girl wearing a crop top with hot pants!

> Like many girls I knew, I had fallen into the habit of wearing jeans all the time during the sixties. In 1970, when I was eighteen, the craze for hot pants hit the scene. Suddenly, we were all emphasising our legs instead of hiding them. It was shocking to some people to see girls walking about showing their legs right up as far as you could go. And when combined with a crop top, you certainly got some looks in the street, as well as wolf whistles and men sounding their car horns. The downside was that quite a few places – pubs, shops and so on – would not allow women in dressed like that. For some, it was deemed indecent to dress that way. (Pat Howard)

Maxi skirts also enjoyed a vogue around this time among some girls. Hemlines in skirts had moved up and down during the course of the twentieth century. In Edwardian times, they had brushed the floor and then risen and fallen with the passing decades. By the mid-1960s, they had settled somewhere around the knee. The miniskirt changed that, with skirts becoming as short as a woman dared to wear them. In the 1970s a sudden reversal took place, with many girls choosing to wear skirts which reached down to their ankles.

> I loved the maxi skirt. It was so feminine and entirely different from what had been going on in fashions for the previous few years. Like many teenage girls I had favoured jeans for a while, with the occasional pair of hot pants. Neither was really feminine, nor very elegant. The maxi skirt harked back to an earlier age and it was a pleasure to enter a room with my skirt swishing round my ankles. I was sorry when they went out of fashion again a couple of years later. (Maria T. Valentine)

What was happening with young men's fashion while hot pants and maxi skirts came and went? At the start of the decade, the androgynous look was still going strong. This was a time when both jeans and tops were being tie-dyed, a process that was usually undertaken at home.

> I remember Dylon dyes. They came in little aluminium drums that you had to puncture. I know that salt was needed to fix the colours once they had been dyed, and I also remember my mother going mad because the dyes always ran and she ended up doing my clothes separately. We used bleach as well, but only on blue jeans. Unless you were very careful, the overall effect was pretty frightful and some of us persuaded our art teacher at college to let us use the facilities there for our tie-dyeing, on the grounds that it was practically art anyway. We did batik as well there, dripping hot wax on clothes and then dying them. (Mick Parker)

> Some people had the knack of tie-dye and others did not. I was one of those who never quite mastered the art. My

T-shirts always came out looking muddy and smudged. I had
a friend though who was an absolute whiz at it. We used to
get him to do ours for us. You never see tie-dyed clothes today,
which is not altogether surprising. Looking at photographs
now, it looks really scruffy and not in the least attractive. You
could buy tie-dye stuff in the shops and this always looked
much better than our home-made efforts. (K.A. Silverstone)

Perhaps the archetypal fashion item from the 1970s and
one which has come to symbolise the whole decade, were
flared trousers, or 'flares'. There were few teenage boys
who did not fall victim to this fad. So common was the
wearing of flares by young men that it is worth looking in
detail at the origin of this peculiar style of trousers, which
were closely associated with two other styles of trousers
around at that time; bell-bottoms and loon pants.

In the 1960s, when the wearing of trousers by women
was becoming acceptable, a fashion was devised called
bell-bottoms. These were trousers which appeared to have
been modelled on nineteenth-century sailors' uniforms,
with the trousers flaring out from the calf downwards.
This fashion dropped from sight in the mid-1960s and
then emerged again in the 1970s.

Bell-bottom jeans! They were a big thing in the seventies,
similar to, but not precisely the same, as flares and loon
pants. Boys and girls both wore them and I think everybody
had at least one pair. They were, to begin with, associated
with hippies, but then became popular with anybody who
wished to look up-to-date and stylish. (Geoffrey C. Feldman)

Flares differ from bell-bottoms in that the flaring begins at
the knee, rather than the calf. Jeans in this style were often

very tightly cut right down as far as the knee, to emphasise the flaring. The circumference of the trousers legs at the bottom could be pretty substantial, which gave 1970s teenage boys a most distinctive and wholly bizarre appearance!

> I had one pair of flares which flapped round my ankles and covered my feet almost entirely. I have a couple of photographs taken at about that time and I cannot tell you how weird I look. It was just one of those things that you do solely to keep up with others. I suppose that today's teenagers must have similarly odd fashions, but they don't notice so much. Flares were very obvious. (Chris Arthur)

> When I was at secondary school and started wearing long trousers (around 1966) there was a big division between those who wore turn-ups and those who did not. You never see turn-ups at all these days on trousers, but at that time all smart trousers had them. Trousers without turn-ups were daring and fashionable. After a few years, no young person would have been seen dead wearing turn-ups. Much the same thing happened with flares in the 1970s. Older men who were not in the groove, as it were, might continue to wear straight-cut trousers, but anybody young would want to have flares or bell-bottoms. It was an age thing; teenagers wanted flares and older men were happy to stick to the old-fashioned sort. (Mick Parker)

Flared trousers, like moustaches and shirts left open to expose the chest, now act as a handy visual shorthand for the 1970s. Along with various associated fashions, flares held sway among teenage boys and young men for almost the whole of the decade, before fading away abruptly when the 1980s arrived.

Although, objectively, they look ridiculous, flares still look stylish and sophisticated to me. There was just something about them that told you that the man wearing them was really cool and in the groove; the sort of guy who would be likely to drive a sports car with an 8 Track Stereo in it. I remember myself at nineteen with flares, a shirt with the top buttons undone and a moustache which was just about visible to the naked eye. I have never looked so stylish and probably never will again! (Christopher Walker)

Similar to flares and also considered exceedingly cool were loon pants, which were a special type of bell-bottom casual trousers. Short for 'balloon pants', at first these could only be acquired by mail order from a company which advertised on the back page of the *New Musical Express*. To begin with, loon pants were only worn by hippies but the style soon became popular with many young people. Versions of loon pants became available not just by mail order, but at markets all over the country. In the second half of the decade, they became associated with the disco movement.

I loved my bell-bottom jeans, but by 1985 they were definitely out of style. By that time, when I was twenty-one, they had become the object of remark and far from making me look stylish, I was looking like Rip Van Winkle. (Paul Clarke)

Does anybody still wear loon pants? I remember having to save up to order a pair from *NME*. I was something of a trend-setter, I suppose, because I had loon pants before any of my friends. They were usually worn with a tie-dye vest and sandals. Although at first it was mainly freaks wearing them, they looked so cool that an awful lot of teenagers

wanted them. This led to various companies turning out
cheap bootleg copies which you could pick up cheap in
places like Camden market. By 1972, everyone was wearing them and those who wanted to be leaders in fashion
had to look elsewhere. (David Ford)

If flares were the hallmark of the fashionable male teenager of the 1970s, platform shoes were the corresponding
feature for girls. This particular item of clothing spanned
the decade with uncanny precision, beginning in 1970 and
falling from grace in 1979.

You can pretty well date a picture showing young women
in platform shoes. I remember that they appeared suddenly in magazines like *Petticoat* in 1970. They seemed
to come from nowhere and yet within a year or two, every
teenage girl with any pretensions to being fashionable had
to have a pair. Then they became deeply unfashionable
overnight in 1979 and vanished even more quickly than
they had appeared. (Theresa O. Littlestone)

For many years, in this country there has been a tradition for women to wear footwear which appears to make
them taller than is actually the case. The platform shoe
was a natural development of this idea and in retrospect
it is surprising that it took so long for somebody to come
up with the idea of a shoe which raised the height of a
woman not just from the heel but along the whole length
of her foot. Of course, the higher the platform, the more
akin to walking on stilts the experience of wearing this
type of footwear became. There were sprained, even
broken ankles and regular incidents of teenage girls
falling down stairs, sometimes even in front of traffic,

because they could barely totter more than a few paces
in the things.

> Learning to walk in platforms was like starting to ride a
> bike. Most girls are used to walking in high heels, with
> only the back of the foot raised. Platform shoes are a
> different thing entirely and until you are used to them it
> is very easy to trip up because you have misjudged the
> position of your foot. I never hurt myself, but a friend
> ended up falling over after a few drinks and spraining her
> ankle. You might get the hang of the things when you
> were sober, but after you had been to the pub it could be
> a different thing altogether. (Mary A. Barker)

The platform shoe had a sole which was at least four
inches thick. Later on, these soles were combined with
heels that were even higher. These really were a menace,
as was demonstrated by the model Naomi Campbell in
the 1990s – she was defeated by a pair of platforms with
five-inch soles and nine-inch heels and ended up sprawling
across the catwalk during a fashion show.

> Some time around 1978, when I was fifteen, I begged my
> mother to get me platforms with high heels. She did in the
> end as a birthday present. I could only wear them for walking
> short distances, because even stepping down from the kerb
> to cross the road was a tricky business. I took a couple of
> tumbles, luckily not while walking along the platform on the
> underground or anything like that. You really needed circus
> skills to walk up stairs in the things. (Maria T. Valentine)

Platform shoes became a cultural icon of the 1970s due
to their adoption by some glam rock stars, which served

massively to increase their desirability among teenagers. In 1975, the film of the rock opera *Tommy* was released. Elton John starred as the mythic hero, the Pinball Wizard. For this role he wore platform shoes which were modelled upon the Dr Marten boots so beloved of skinheads. These boots were an astonishing four and a half feet high and Elton John had to be strapped into them with metal callipers. This image served to fix in the minds of many of platforms being a defining fashion of the 1970s.

> It is the first thing I think of when I remember being a teenager, wearing platforms. My boyfriends all wore flares and I was tottering along on ludicrously high platform shoes. I cannot tell you how awful I looked, wearing hot pants and platforms. (Sarah P. Moran)

To begin with, as with so many quirky fashions, platform shoes were the exclusive province of teenagers. In 1971 you would have been hard pressed to find anybody over the age of twenty wearing platforms. By the late 1970s, however, they were being worn by women of all ages and even a few young men. They enjoyed a late blooming around 1977, with the disco fashions inspired by films like *Saturday Night Fever*.

Disco dancing was a reaction to rock music, and this style of music enjoyed great popularity in the second half of the 1970s. Couples would go through elaborate dance routines and the men dressed very elegantly, often in three-piece suits (in *Saturday Night Fever*, John Travolta famously wore a white three-piece suit). Platform shoes and boots were sometimes worn by male dancers as another way of drawing attention to their flamboyant appearance.

I remember going out dancing wearing a suit and platform boots. I used to get a cab to such events, because I wouldn't have wanted to walk the streets or get on a bus looking like that. It might have been alright on an American film, but for an eighteen-year-old boy in East London, to parade the streets like that would have been inviting at best ridicule and at worst physical violence. (Terrry Barlow)

The demise of both platform shoes and loon pants, and also bell-bottoms among British teenagers, was caused, as is so often the case with teenage culture in this country, by events in the United States. It is curious to see how a relatively minor event in Chicago in 1979 should have brought to a sudden end teenage enthusiasm for this style of dress.

The disco scene in America was an underground one for most of the early 1970s. When the dancing and the music which was connected with it became hugely popular on both sides of the Atlantic in the late 1970s, many rock fans were outraged and T-shirts appeared claiming, 'Disco sucks'. Some were even less complimentary. Groups like the Bee Gees and the Jackson Brothers came to be viewed as the very antithesis of the rock scene which had, until then, enjoyed unrivalled success in both the American and British charts.

Along with the music went a sartorial style. Loon pants, bell-bottoms and platform shoes were a part of this and after a year or two became inextricably linked, in the minds of many, with disco music. Few of those teenagers who wore loon pants or platform shoes were even aware of the controversy which was about to erupt in America in 1979 and bring an end to a whole fashion scene here.

The summer of 1979 was really the height of disco fever. In this country, teenagers were wearing bell-bottoms, loon pants and flares, platform shoes were everywhere and there was something of a trend for disco music, with the Bee Gees being especially favoured. There were mutterings of discontent in America among rock fans and several music magazines had begun printing vitriolic attacks on the disco craze. As July began, the top six records in the American music charts were all disco songs. The situation was mirrored in this country.

On July 12th, an event was organised in Chicago for the interval of an important baseball game. It was billed as 'Disco Demolition Night'. A leading DJ had arranged to rig explosives up to a crate of disco records and blow them up. Incredibly, this was allowed to go ahead and in the resulting riot, fires were lit and the police cleared the ground.

By September 1979, there were no disco songs at all in the American charts and many radio stations avoided playing black and Latin music in case they were seen as favouring disco over rock. A consequence of this was that any clothing or fashions which had been associated with disco quickly became unfashionable overnight. In Britain, teenagers abandoned their platform shoes and bell-bottom jeans, as well as rejecting disco music, just as fans of popular music in America were doing. This single event had a major influence upon 1970s' music and fashion in this country and really served to bring down the curtain on some of the most iconic styles of the decade. By 1980, you would have had your work cut out to see a pair of bell-bottoms or platforms anywhere in the country!

The music that teenagers listened to, the clothes they wore and the films they watched during the 1970s were not isolated phenomena occurring in a vacuum. They were all manifestations of what was taking place in society as a whole. Children and teenagers, though, are famously more prone to falling prey to fads and crazes than adults.

Sometimes, the fashion for something would take off almost literally overnight; platform shoes were one such craze. They were more or less unknown in this country until the teenage girls' magazine *Seventeen* ran a piece about them in 1970. That year saw an explosion of popularity for the things, which lasted for almost ten years. Much the same thing happened with loon pants, another common item of clothing at the time. The only source at first was a mail order company advertising in the *New Musical Express*. Being seen in a newspaper read by teenagers was enough in itself to get the fashion going.

The girls' magazine *Jackie* was another source of fashion for teenagers. Each issue, they would run illustrated pieces on what the 'with it' girl was wearing. It is debateable to what extent they were objectively describing trends in clothing and how much they were in fact creating them. Just as with *Seventeen* and platform shoes, *Jackie* prided itself on being a leader in fashion rather than merely a mirror or barometer.

I used to get *Jackie* and it was one way that we knew how to dress and what was fashionable. In October 1975, for instance, they had a bit about skirts and every single one of the skirts they showed was ankle length. You knew from this that maxi skirts were in and minis definitely out. The following summer, in 1976, the fashion pages had nothing but bell-bottoms and knee-length skirts. You knew by that that maxis were out and that you had best buy some bell-bottom jeans! (Maria T. Valentine)

4

Alcohol and Drugs

It is impossible to determine whether teenagers of the 1970s drank more, less, or the same amount as teenagers of today. In most instances, the majority of teenagers exaggerate about their consumption of alcohol and in some cases, the use of illegal drugs. Some boastfully proclaim to be drinking a bottle of whisky a day, while others claim to be teetotallers.

> I know that as a teenager I used to drink at parties and so on. I couldn't say how many units that was though or how many days in the week. I have an idea that in the seventies, teenagers usually only drank at the weekend. I also think that it was pretty uncommon to see anybody the worse for wear for drink at that time. Along the high road in the town where I now live, it is full of drunken young people on Saturday nights. Many, perhaps most of them, look to me to be in their later teens or early twenties. I know for a fact that I didn't see anything of that sort when I was a teenager. Sometimes you might find one person who would overdo it a bit, but you certainly would not witness groups of a dozen or so all drunk. (Geoffrey C. Feldman)

What is certain is that it was in the 1970s that many teenagers first began to experiment with illegal drugs, in addition to drinking alcohol. The use of substances like cannabis and LSD had spread to this country from America in the late 1960s, but took a little while to become popular. At first, they were the preserve of wealthy rock stars, but gradually the smoking of dope and dropping of acid became a weekend activity for practically any teenager in this country who felt like indulging in them. By any standards, the price of the recreational drugs used by teenagers from the early 1970s onwards was incredibly low. In 1972, for instance, the accepted price of one dose of LSD, or a 'tab of acid' as it was universally known, was a mere 50p. The most common amount of cannabis bought for personal consumption was the so-called 'quid deal'; prices like these put drugs within the financial reach of almost all teenagers.

> I'm not sure how common it was for young people to experiment with drugs in the 1970s. One or two of the people I knew used to smoke dope from time to time, but that was about the limit of it. When my son was at secondary school, he told me that some of the boys used to smoke cannabis during the lunch hour. This was when he was fifteen, in 1994. I can't imagine anything like that happening at school when I was that age. Dope used to be seen as definitely illegal and smoking it was a pretty clandestine affair. Hard to imagine in 1974, having a joint on school premises! (Katherine Cassidy)

Illegal Drugs

Throughout the 1960s there was some use of recreational drugs in this country, and from the beginning, the use of drugs was associated with young people. By 1970, cannabis was freely available in Britain's bigger cities, and a year or two later so too was LSD, known universally as 'acid'. Other drugs were appearing on the scene, but in the early 1970s it was cannabis and LSD which were being used most by teenagers.

> When I was fifteen, a group of friends were all smoking dope and doing acid a lot. I had tried them both before I was sixteen. I think that girls used to do drugs like that a bit younger than the boys, because we typically hung round with young men who were three or four years older than us. I turned sixteen in 1974 and by that time I was a bit tired of the whole dope thing. It would start off with a joint before we went out somewhere and then before you knew it the evening had slipped by and we were still sitting there getting stoned and had not decided where we would be going. I never took much to acid either. A lot of it was cut with speed and used to make one feel terrible after the trip was over. (Anon)

The division between those who used drugs and those who preferred alcohol was based partly upon social class. The use of illegal drugs in this country had been pioneered by middle-class students and hippies. They were, at the start of the 1970s, more likely to be taken by teenagers from middle-class backgrounds than any other. By the end of the decade, the smoking of cannabis was common among all socio-economic classes, but in 1970 alcohol was still the chosen drug of most working-class youths. There was a kind of snobbishness about the whole business. Middle-class students sometimes claimed that cannabis was superior to alcohol, the recreational drug which they associated with their parents' generation. Cannabis supposedly made one mellow and thoughtful, rather than rowdy and irrational.

We felt a kind of contempt for those who preferred to get drunk at the weekends, instead of getting stoned. They would stagger around, throwing up and getting into arguments, while we sat in a candlelit room listening to Kevin Ayers while passing round a joint. We thought that our conversation was really deep and meaningful, but I daresay that it was just as silly and shallow as that taking place in the pub. (Christopher Walker)

There was a saying that we took to our hearts – this was about 1971/72 – which was that alcohol provoked paroxysms of folly, but that cannabis provoked paroxysms of wisdom. This tied in neatly with what we had already decided – that smoking made us a cut above the kids down the pub. (Martin O'Connell)

For many working-class teenagers, rejecting the use of drugs was also a declaration of sorts. In their minds it was connected with lazy dropouts, not working people like themselves. They accordingly chose to stick with the familiar; alcohol over cannabis and LSD.

We all used to go to the pub, especially on Fridays and Saturdays. The boys that I knocked around with had no time at all for drugs. We had what you might describe as traditional views, even though we were only in our late teens. Drugs were what long-haired hippy layabouts were mixed up in and we wanted no part of it. I honestly believe that if we had heard of anybody selling drugs locally, we would either have roughed him up or called the police. This was the early seventies. A few years later, maybe 1980, and everybody was a lot more relaxed about drugs; well, dope at any rate. (Anon)

The 1970s were the time when illegal drugs changed from being a defining characteristic of the hippy movement, into being something that many teenagers did for relaxation at weekends, in much the same way that their parents might enjoy a glass of whiskey.

> When I first dropped acid in 1971, it was an unusual thing to do. Some of my friends smoked dope but none of them had ever taken acid. It was not available as freely as cannabis. Five years later, when I was nineteen, it was all over the place and most people I knew had tried it at least once. The reason I took it when I was so young was that my boyfriend at the time was always smoking and often tripping. It seemed an interesting thing to do. By the end of the seventies, you could buy the stuff anywhere and it was no longer a novelty. (Polly Reynolds)

Something which has changed dramatically since the 1970s is the effect upon teenagers of being caught in possession of drugs like cannabis. These days, police policy differs from that of the 1970s; even when young people are found to be smoking dope, action is rarely taken. In the modern scheme of things, a teenager being found with a small amount of cannabis might reasonably expect to escape arrest entirely, particularly in larger cities. This was not at all the case forty years ago.

> When I was seventeen – this was 1971 – me and a few friends used to meet from time to time and go to the local park to smoke. None of our parents would have tolerated dope smoking in their houses. The three of us were sitting there one afternoon when a young guy walked past and then came back again. He asked for the joint we were smoking and, like an idiot, I handed it to him. I thought that he just wanted a drag. He then signalled to a clump of trees and three uniformed officer emerged and arrested us. Apparently they had heard

that a group of teenagers were in the habit of smoking in the
park and had staked out the place. All for three seventeen-year-
olds smoking dope! We were fined £100 each, which works
out at well over £1,000 at today's values, a staggeringly large
amount for just enough dope to make a single joint. (Anon)

I was arrested at a festival with a very small amount of dope;
enough for a couple of joints. My father had to come up to
Windsor to sign bail for me. This was 1972 and the solici-
tor he hired warned us that there was a real chance that I
would be sent to prison. The magistrates in Windsor were
notoriously tough on drugs at that time, particularly when
the famous Windsor Free Festival was running. (Anon)

In the 1970s many adults honestly believed that cannabis
was on a par with heroin, and that once their teenage son or
daughter began smoking dope it was only a matter of time
before they were injecting themselves with hard drugs. The
police and courts noted with alarm the spread of drug use
among young people and felt that if determined action were
taken to nip this menace in the bud, then it might be possible to reverse the use of 'soft' drugs, like cannabis, through
harsh enough penalties. It was, as we can see in retrospect, a
policy doomed to failure. Today, cannabis use among teenagers is, if not tolerated by society, at least accepted as just
another of those things which young people do.

A couple of years ago, I caught wind of the fact that my son
was smoking dope in his bedroom. I spoke to him about it
and explained the harm that a criminal conviction might
bring him, as well as the fact that I didn't really want it
happening in my house. The whole thing was relaxed and
good natured and as far as I know had the desired effect.

If my father had found *me* taking drugs, I think he would have marched me to the police station; he was that fierce about the whole business. (Anon)

Drugs and Music

In 1970, illegal drugs were mainly associated with hippies. Teenagers who smoked cannabis and dropped LSD were likely to have long hair and dress in an unconventional fashion. This particular group of teenagers and young people claimed that the use of drugs enhanced the experience of listening to pop music. They would smoke dope in communes while listening to bands such as Country Joe and the Fish or Soft Machine; maintaining that it was only when stoned that they could fully appreciate the lyrics of the songs. LSD was felt to make listening to music more enjoyable also, and turn it from a casual relaxation into a deep and meaningful experience.

I had a friend whose parents used to work a lot and so he often had the house to himself. We used to smoke in his bedroom while listening to Crosby Stills, Roy Harper and so on. The words of the songs sounded very deep and meaningful when we were stoned. This was a big thing for our group; just smoking dope and listening to music. It was the whole thing, the music, passing the joint; it was a large part of what connected us. Of course, if you listen to those same songs today, without being stoned, they sound pretty feeble. Take the track from Crosby Still's album, 'déjà vu'. This came out in 1970 and we used to listen to it all the time. Try this for banality: 'Almost cut my hair, it happened just the other day, you could have said it was in my way'. Like I said, you really had to be stoned to appreciate stuff like that! (Mick Parker)

I used to listen to music a lot when I was stoned and so did
many of my friends. The lyrics really did have more meaning
after a couple of joints. Many of these songs had messages
anyway, more so than is the case today. A lot of singers at
that time had something to say about important issues. Just
think about 'After the Gold Rush' by Neil Young. The title
track is about pollution and the exhaustion of the Earth's
mineral resources. Not all songs were as heavy as that, but
many were concerned about politics and racism. This is
seldom the case today and I can't think that listening to much
modern pop music would be a more enlightening experience
when stoned. (Anon)

At live concerts and festivals, drugs would be offered for
sale and consumed pretty freely. The festival goer who
turned down a pull on a joint would be eyed askance,
as though he might be an undercover police officer! This
use of drugs at concerts spread throughout the 1970s
until it turned into the norm for many teenagers. This
generation, who are now in their forties, fifties and
sixties, are the parents and grandparents of today. No
wonder society now has a rather more laid-back attitude
to the use of recreational drugs; the chances are that
many teenagers today have older relatives who smoked
dope at least once.

I feel hypocritical when I lecture my children about drugs.
I tell them all the dangers of ecstasy and how one thing can
lead to another, but the one thing I don't tell them is that
I used to smoke dope all the time when I was sixteen or
seventeen. If they knew this, I am afraid that it would just
confirm their belief that it is OK to take drugs. After all, it
doesn't seem to have done me any harm. (Anon)

Of course, none of this is to suggest that all teenagers in the 1970s were taking drugs regularly, only that as the decade progressed, the use of illegal drugs by young people became more and more widespread until it was scarcely remarkable to hear that this or that teenager had been known to have had a drag of a joint. That this is the case may be seen by the various politicians who were teenagers during the 1970s and who admit that they too smoked dope at college or university.

> It would have been a rare student when I was at university from 1973-76 who did not at least try dope once. It was everywhere in the university and you could not have gone to a party without being handed a joint. Not everybody took to it; it is certainly an acquired taste. Many people felt giddy and sick when they first tried it, especially if they weren't used to smoking ordinary cigarettes. Nevertheless, I didn't know anybody who had never had a puff at all while they were at university. I would guess that anybody, politician, bishop or anyone else who was at university in the seventies, has at least tried dope. (Christopher Walker)

By the time that the 1980s arrived, smoking cannabis was no longer restricted to any particular teenage subculture. It was freely available all over the place and many young people were using it in addition to, rather than instead of, alcohol.

> Dope was always around, even if you didn't want it. You might go to a pub and somebody would ask if you wanted to score, or be at a party and see people smoking. It was a rare weekend where I did not come across dope at all. I have no idea if it is still like that today with teenagers. Maybe they have more sense. (Maria T. Valentine)

Alcohol

The favourite drug of teenagers in this country has, for at least 2,000 years, not been cannabis or LSD but alcohol. However, the most obvious difference between today and the 1970s is the availability of alcohol to teenagers. Pubs have always been more or less strict about not serving those who are under the age of eighteen. After all, they stand to lose their licences if they are caught allowing younger teenagers to drink on their premises. This has not changed much over the last few decades. What has changed is the way that alcohol is now widely available in many places other than public houses. Let us see how things were in the 1970s for teenagers hoping to get drunk.

> I sometimes wonder how teenagers today manage to get hold of enough booze to get drunk. The pubs near where I lived did not like having young people in them and would pretend not to believe that we were eighteen, up I suppose to the age of twenty or so. This meant getting drink from off-licences, but they were few and far between. We didn't have too much money, so it would often end up with a group of two or three of us sharing a quart of cider; hardly enough to get paralytic on! There simply weren't as many places selling alcohol in the mid-seventies as there are today. (Geoffrey C. Feldman)

> In the seventies, you had to hunt out alcohol if you wanted to buy it. It was not on sale in supermarkets and corner shops. Anybody walking round a supermarket today is reminded of the stuff, it is everywhere. When I was a teenager, there were only a couple of off-licences near to where I lived and they were both a mile or so from my home. You had to go out of your way to get hold of it and I think this made us drink less. (Chris Arthur)

I certainly wasn't a teetotaller when I was in my teens, but at the same time, it was not uncommon for me to go for weeks without touching the stuff. This was the case even when I was eighteen or nineteen. If we went to a pub, I would have a drink, but that was about it. It would have been seen as a bit odd for us to go out and buy drink to consume at home. Drinking was really a social activity in the seventies, the aim was not to get blind drunk for the sake of it. I really think that if any friend had suggested that we buy some alcohol and then deliberately become intoxicated, we would have given her a funny look. It just wasn't what we did then. (Esther M. Hannigan)

We are so used to seeing all sorts of alcohol on sale in supermarkets and corner shops that it comes as a bit of a shock to realise that until the 1970s, off-licences were most commonly attached to pubs. The same rules applied when buying alcohol from them as were applied when trying to get served in the pub itself. In other words, unless you were very clearly over the age of eighteen there was no chance of getting so much as a bottle of beer.

The only off-licence near to where I lived was one attached to the pub. When you went in, a bell rang and one of the bar staff came out to serve. Of course, the problem was that these people were used to refusing to serve anybody trying to buy a drink in the pub if they looked a day under eighteen and they behaved the same way when you went into the off-licence. This was in the early seventies, before supermarkets and corner shops began selling booze. The offies kept the same opening hours as pubs as well, which meant that even if you were eighteen, if you wanted a can of beer in the morning or on a Sunday afternoon, you were out of luck. Because teenagers aren't famous for planning ahead, it meant that we often

found ourselves with no alcohol and no prospect of getting any
until the evening. I'm sure that this had the effect of making us
drink less, even if we'd had the money. (Mick Parker)

There were also very strict licensing laws too, which
restricted the hours that alcohol could be sold. In general,
one could only buy alcohol during the hours that pubs were
serving it. At that time, pubs did not open until lunchtime
and closed during the afternoon. This meant that it was not
possible to obtain alcohol at all for much of the day, and
these restrictions meant that it was a lot trickier for teenagers to get hold of alcoholic drinks than is the case today.

Drinking used to be something which was limited to parties
and pubs, simply because you didn't see alcohol all over the
place the way you do today. You had to make a special effort
to seek it out. When I was a teenager, buying alcohol was more
of a business. You didn't see it on display and you had to find
an off license selling the stuff. Even then, many off-licences
were ferociously cautious about age and until I was twenty, I
was being asked for identification. (Katherine Cassidy)

The other factor which worked to discourage heavy drinking in teenagers was the price. In 1974, a bottle of vodka
from the off-licence cost around £2.50. In modern terms,
this works out at about £25. Today, you can buy the same
bottle of vodka for less than £10. In other words, you can
buy almost three times as much alcohol for your money
now, compared to forty years ago. Some strong ciders provide even more alcohol for your money than spirits do.

I don't really remember me or any of my friends actually setting out to get drunk during the seventies. It happened from

time to time because, obviously, we weren't as used to drinking as older people and could misjudge the strength of drinks, but it wasn't the object of the exercise. I know that today, teenagers will announce that they are going to get 'hammered' or 'bladdered', and that is their intention before the evening even begins. This was not something that anybody would have said forty years ago when I was first drinking. We wanted to be sophisticated and copy adult behaviour. (Martin O'Connell)

Alcohol was much more expensive forty years ago and it was also far harder to get hold of. Most teenagers could only afford to drink alcohol once or twice a week. Even then, those occasions tended not to be what we now call 'binge drinking' but just having a few drinks at a party or with friends in the pub. There was overindulgence, as there has always been with teenagers and alcohol, but the aim was not to drink one's self into a mindless stupor. True, this might happen after a party or a long evening at the pub, but it would be in the nature of an unexpected event, not as the avowed intent of those going out to the pub.

One difference that is very noticeable from now is that in the seventies, it was extremely rare to see a drunken girl or woman. For a woman to get into the sort of state in which one sometimes saw men, that is to say incapable of walking because of drink, was seen as disgusting and unfeminine; especially by older people. Even amongst my friends, a girl who got drunk would be liable to get a 'reputation'. It wasn't what boys wanted to see in a girl who they were thinking of asking out. Now I suppose that this is sheer sexism, after all, there is no earthly reason why it should be any worse for a girl to get drunk than it is for a man. I hear teenage girls in the pub today talking and they will refer loudly to having been pissed or 'out of their heads'. The way they talk one gets the impression that this is by way of being a regular event and that they use precisely the same language to talk about it as do boys. I suppose this is the so-called 'ladette culture'. When I was a teenager, say thirty-five years ago, not only did girls seldom get drunk; they had a completely different set of expressions to cover the event. They might, for instance, talk of 'getting tiddly'. This is and was an entirely feminine expression; no young man would refer to having been 'tiddly'. Or a girl might say that she had had a little too much the previous night. The whole culture was that it was not acceptable for a girl to get drunk and that if she did it was something to be apologetic about. (David Ford)

Two factors combined to make drinking a considerably civilised affair for teenagers in the 1970s. There was little or no binge drinking, hardly any drunkenness among girls, and what drinking there was was confined to pubs and parties. Of course, some young people had too much to drink, but this was a cause for regret.

Me and my mates used to go out drinking and we might get pretty lively. It was not unknown for us to have too much and even for somebody to fall over or end up sleeping it off out of doors. Such things were not common though and it was seen as being a sign of somebody who 'couldn't hold his drink'. That's an expression that you don't hear very often these days. I know young boys who boast now of falling over, stupid drunk, whereas forty years ago, they would have felt sheepish about it. (Chris Arthur)

For various reasons, partly connected with cost, partly with the ready availability of liquor, and partly by society's disapproval, public drunkenness was viewed, until a few decades ago, as being an unedifying and, to many, a disgusting sight.

5

Sex

For the first three quarters or so of the twentieth century, extra-marital or pre-marital sex was severely frowned upon in this country. This meant that the easiest way for teenagers to have an active sex life was to get married young; which was one of the main motivations behind the marriages of sixteen and seventeen year olds. Powerful disincentives were at work to discourage teenagers from being sexually active before marriage. Chief of these was the possibility of an unwanted pregnancy, which was regarded as little short of a catastrophe for a single girl. For boys too, the consequences could be serious. The so-called shotgun wedding was still going strong at the beginning of the 1970s, and many teenage boys found themselves being coerced into an unexpectedly early marriage as a result of getting a girl 'into trouble', as the saying went.

I was sleeping with my girlfriend in 1971 and she was on the pill. It was not as widely used then as it is now. Anyway, she used to carry it round in her handbag; she was scared of her parents seeing it in her room. They found out one day

that we were having sex and although we had been thinking
of getting engaged, that clinched it. Her father was furious
about it and we announced the engagement soon afterwards
and got married the following year, when we were both
eighteen. I think he had the idea that now that his daughter
was no longer a virgin, no other man would want to marry
her. Even then, this was a pretty old-fashioned view. (Anon)

If my parents had known that I was sleeping with my boyfriend
then I would have come under pressure to become engaged to
him. A single girl having sex without any intention of marriage
was a shocking idea to many older people in the early seventies. Things eased up a little by 1980, but in 1970 you would be
running the risk of getting a very bad reputation once people
knew that you were willing to go 'all the way' with a boy and
then not want to get engaged or anything. (Pat Howard)

As a result of all this, sex between teenagers up until the
mid-1960s was often a furtive, hole-and-corner affair, frequently falling short of full intercourse. The frantic desire
to avoid having an illegitimate baby became idealised as a
desire on the part of young girls to remain 'pure' and 'save
themselves' for their husband.

We used to talk about 'saving ourselves' for our husbands.
Remaining a virgin until your wedding day was a big thing. Not
all of us managed it, but it was something a lot of girls hoped for.
It was just about OK to sleep with a boy if you were engaged, but
otherwise it was something you might do but keep quiet about.
You might tell your best friend, but nobody else. There was very
definitely a double standard operating, which meant that girls
who had sex with their boyfriends were seen as 'easy'. This was
not at all a good thing to be viewed as. (Katherine Cassidy)

This meant that various sexual acts could be countenanced, provided that they would not lead to pregnancy.

> Without going into the gory details, my girlfriend would let me do practically anything I wanted, as long as it did not involve actual intercourse. She was determined to 'save herself for marriage', as she put it. Even at the time, which would have been either 1969 or 1970, I thought this was the height of hypocrisy. Nevertheless, she was not the only one engaging in such mental gymnastics. By exchanging notes with friends, it was plain that their girlfriends were playing much the same game. There was a superstitious regard for virginity, which was defined in a very narrow sense. (Chris Arthur)

Sexual morality is very different today from how it was in the 1970s and for this we must thank, or blame, the teenagers of the time, according to whether or not we think that those changes have been a blessing or a curse. Virginity before marriage is no longer the prized asset that it once was, and it is more common than not for couples to live together before they get married. All this is a direct consequence of what was called the 'sexual revolution', a battle which teenagers fought valiantly throughout the decade!

> My daughter made no particular secret of the fact that she was sleeping with various boyfriends. This was in the nineties and it was something which had, by then, come to be taken for granted. Even her father knew about it, although I don't think that she actually told him. This is breathtakingly different from the way things were when I was a teenager myself. I was on the pill and sleeping with my boyfriend, but my father would have gone absolutely mad if he'd known. At the very least, he would have barred my boyfriend from the

house and very possibly have threatened him with violence.
I used to carry the pill round with me because I wasn't sure
that my mother didn't snoop round my bedroom when
I was out. This was when I was eighteen. (Anon)

By the 1980s, a lot had changed in sexual morality generally. There was more divorce, there was the impression that
more people were being unfaithful to their partners and
engaging in adultery, and it was more common for young
people to sleep together before they were married. The way
it seemed to me was that this relaxation of sexual rules
began with teenagers and kind of spread outwards from
them. They were the trailblazers and as they abandoned the
rules, older people just followed suit. (Mary A. Barker)

Morality in sexual matters was oppressive for both young
men and women, which resulted in many teenagers marrying young. It also discouraged them from separating. With
the advent of effective contraception, which a woman
could control for herself, the stage was set for general
sexual liberation. Before that time, the basic rule had been
that sex was only permissible within marriage. Of course
there was adultery and pre-marital sexual activity, but the
rules were still acknowledged and those who transgressed
them expected to incur penalties, which they almost invariably did, once they were detected in such acts.

If an unmarried girl had a baby in 1970, it would have
been a cause for shame and embarrassment. Some parents
would have chucked her out, and at the very least, the
neighbours would have disapproved. It would have been an
'illegitimate baby'; a bastard, born out of wedlock. I don't think
I knew anybody in that position in those days. It was taken

absolutely for granted that you didn't have a baby unless you
were married, or at the very least planning to get married.
Adultery, too, was frowned upon and could lead to people
being ostracised. This culture of disapproval helped to preserve
family structures. It was tough on those who were caught out,
and they were usually the women in the case. (Sarah P. Moran)

During the 1970s, many teenagers rejected the 'rules' that
older people followed on questions relating to sex and
marriage. Sex before, outside or even instead of marriage
became widely accepted among young people. By the end
of the decade, this relaxation in morality had spread outwards and become the norm, and not just among teenagers
and young adults. Marriage became an optional extra and
could be abandoned if it was found not to suit.

The Pill

During the 1970s, such attitudes as those discussed above
underwent a dramatic transformation. One of the most
significant factors leading to these changing mores was not
philosophical, religious or sociological, but chemical. In
1961, oral contraceptives became available to women in
Britain. There were many ethical debates about 'the pill',
leading to the Catholic Church banning it entirely, describing it as unnatural and contrary to God's will. Many
doctors in this country at first refused to have anything to
do with it, and those who were prepared to prescribe it
would only do so for married woman.

I wanted to go on the pill when I was seventeen. My boyfriend and I were doing it regularly and it just seemed the
most convenient way of taking precautions. I went to my

doctor and he refused outright, saying that he had a personal policy of not giving it to unmarried girls. In any case,
he had known me and my parents since I was born and I
think that he was scandalised at the idea of pre-marital sex.
I had to go to a clinic to get it in the end. (Anon)

By 1970, the pill was acceptable but not commonly used.
It was not until 1974 (when it became available free of
charge) that the use of oral contraceptives mushroomed.
In that year, fewer than 10 per cent of women were 'on the
pill'. Five years later, at the end of the 1970s, the figure was
over 36 per cent and rising. It is debateable to what extent
the pill caused a relaxation of sexual morality or how far
it was merely reflecting what was already happening. What
is indisputable is that whereas in 1970 many teenage girls
refused to sleep with their boyfriends, ten years later an
awful lot more of them of them were prepared to do so.

In 1970, when I was fourteen, the attitudes to sex held by
many women of my mother's age were positively Victorian.
A lot of their ideals hinged around what 'nice' girls would
and wouldn't do; chief of these things was 'letting a man
have what he wanted'. We were led to believe that if we did
this, then the man would not respect us. Men might want to
sow their wild oats, but they didn't want to marry a girl who
would 'give herself' to them before the wedding. There was a
lot of talk about how a man would not respect you if you let
him do it. (Polly Reynolds)

One change that the pill brought about in the 1970s was
that many young girls now felt under pressure to have
sex. It was widely assumed in some circles that any girl
who did not wish to avail herself of this new-found

freedom from the risk of pregnancy must be 'repressed' or 'frigid'.

> I didn't actually want to go to bed with my boyfriend. I thought things were going fine as they were and I was really planning to 'save myself for marriage', as they used to say then. This was 1978 and staying a virgin until your wedding day was beginning to seem a bit quaint and old-fashioned. All the other couples we knew were sleeping together and he just couldn't see why I wouldn't want to. It wasn't as though there was a risk of getting pregnant any more. In the end, I gave in. It wasn't really such a big deal; I wasn't vehemently opposed to the idea of having sex with him. Even so, if it hadn't been for the easy availability of the pill, I probably wouldn't have done it. I would have cited being afraid of getting pregnant as a reason. (Anon)

Free Love

Many of the ideas embodied in the 'alternative society', the lifestyle promoted by the hippies, have now become part of our mainstream culture. One aspect of the alternative lifestyle, or 'counter-culture', was the belief that the existing institutions of society were inherently rotten and caused many problems. Hang-ups about sex were alleged to be particularly damaging, especially to women. Germaine Greer's *The Female Eunuch*, first published in 1970, explored the notion that women should reject celibacy and monogamy and rediscover their appetite for sex which, according to Greer, had been repressed by a patriarchal society.

> At university in the mid-seventies, I associated with many feminists who were convinced that having sex whenever

we wanted it was a revolutionary act which would free society. By refusing the conventional roles of boyfriend and girlfriend, husband and wife, we would be creating a new type of society. Sexual hang-ups were talked of as a very bad thing for women. Unfortunately, this meant that those who really didn't want to have sex were sometimes treated as being victims of psychological problems. Supposedly, all healthy women wanted a fulfilling sex life without any ties and if you weren't doing it with various people then you were not truly liberated. (Christopher Walker)

All this created an atmosphere in which many teenage girls, even those who did not wish to, felt that it was almost their duty to have sex with anybody at all, whenever they wanted. Needless to say, male hippies and many students encouraged this 'liberated' point of view and sexual activity began to be seen as something not merely to be indulged in *before* marriage but *instead* of marriage. Indeed, the nuclear family was seen as one of those institutions that must be brought down at any cost and sexual freedom seemed to be one way of going about the job. It is no wonder that many teenagers embraced this ideology with messianic fervour.

Everybody was at it all the time in the early seventies, at least that's how I remember it. Having indiscriminate sex was one of the ways of registering your rejection of societal norms. Our parents were still stuck with the idea of sex outside marriage as being something shameful and dirty. To show how different we were, we made a point of having as many different partners as we could. As you might imagine, for an eighteen-year-old boy this was a delightful ideology. In one commune that I visited it was considered bad form to stick with one girl in a monogamous relationship. (K.A. Silverstone)

Gay Teenagers

It seems almost incredible today that up until 1967 all sexual activity between males was absolutely forbidden by law. It was in this year that the Sexual Offences Act legalised some homosexual acts for men, but with a number of stringent limits. The acts must take place in private, involve no more than two men and, crucially for young people at the time, the participants had to be over the age of twenty-one. The age of consent for heterosexual sex at that time was the same as it is now, sixteen. The result of this legislation was that throughout the whole of the 1970s, gay teenagers were unable to express their sexuality without running the risk of arrest; two eighteen year olds could be sent to prison for simply going to bed together in their own homes.

> To be an actively gay teenage boy in the seventies was automatically to be a member of a criminal class. It was an offence for two eighteen-year-old boys to go to bed. It went on, of course, but there was always the fear of being found out or arrested. To be arrested for importuning could still destroy a person at that time. You could lose your job, be chucked out of a flat; it could be a complete disaster. Gay teenagers lived with this threat hanging over their heads all the time and it is not surprising that many of them tried to suppress their natures and get married like everybody else. (Anon)

Forty years ago, disapproval of gays was endemic and this attitude was perfectly acceptable to the great majority of people in the country. Derogatory expressions such as 'nancy boy', 'pansy' or 'poofter' were heard all the time; in pubs, workplaces and on the streets. It was certainly not easy to be a gay teenager during this time.

Even if people suspected that you might be 'one of them', it was fairly OK in the early 1970s as long as you kept quiet about it and were very cautious in whom you confided in. Girls were most understanding, but you really didn't want any other boys to know. I made the mistake of telling one girl at school, who then told her friend, who passed on the news to her boyfriend. From then on, my life at school was a nightmare. In the changing rooms for PE, all the other guys would keep away from me, on the assumption that a gay young man would fancy every boy in sight. I was glad to leave school, mainly because of this. (Anon)

In 1970, the Gay Liberation Front (GLF) was founded during a meeting at the London School of Economics. Although it lasted only a few years (it dissolved in 1974), the influence of the GLF was profound. It was formed at a time when overtly gay young people were liable to be assaulted in the street, not only by skinheads but by other young thugs who were offended by the sight of a gay person. Pubs would eject same-sex teenage couples for such innocuous behaviour as just holding hands and the police operated a system of entrapment, where they would seek out gay people to prosecute. This would be done by sending a physically attractive young police officer in plain clothes to known cruising grounds and then arresting anybody who made an approach to him.

I had a friend who was arrested for soliciting for an immoral purpose. It was a police operation. A very good-looking young officer was sent to a favourite cottage, a men's lavatory. He hung around there, making eye contact with people coming in and generally behaving as though he was on the pull. As soon as my friend smiled at him and indicated an empty cubicle, that was it. Bang, he was nicked. In 1970, having an offence of that sort appear in the local paper had catastrophic consequences, believe me. (Anon)

Powerful forces were at work to pressurise teenagers into concealing their sexuality at this time. It was by no means uncommon for fathers to eject their teenage children from the family home if they discovered them to be practicing homosexuals. Having a gay child was widely regarded as a disgrace; something to be hushed up or hidden. It was a time when 'coming out' was all too often the prelude to packing a suitcase and leaving home.

> I was seventeen when I told my parents that I didn't like girls. I don't think that my father really took it in. For him, that sort of thing was the most disgusting thing in the world. When he finally understood, he told me that I would have to go. My mother pleaded with him, but he was adamant. And so, in 1973, I found myself leaving home and moving to London to stay with a friend, crashing on his floor. I didn't go back and visit my parents for over two years. After a while, my father would talk to me again, but it was understood between us that I must never mention being gay. (Anon)

For many teenage boys, their introduction to the gay scene in the 1970s took the form of hearing about and then visiting one of the cruising grounds, which were predominantly frequented by older gay men looking for quick sexual relief. This would entail brief sexual liaisons behind gravestones or trees, or in a public lavatory. The Gay Liberation Front fought to change this, to make it possible for young people to be open about their sexuality and for society to accept gay people on equal terms. They organised meetings at colleges and universities, as well as social activities ranging from discussion groups to discos. Being gay gradually changed from something to be ashamed of to something of which it was possible to be proud. Gay liberation was also encouraged by the so-called 'underground press'; magazines like *Oz* and *Ink*.

The openly-gay scene, of the sort promoted by the GLF, started in London and spread slowly out to the provinces. For gay teenagers, London was the place to be. This, in part, was responsible for many young gay people, who had been brought up in many small towns, moving to London as soon as they were able to do so. This did not mean that being openly gay in London was entirely safe or that gay teenagers were universally accepted; more that there was at least the chance of it happening in the capital, whereas in some small villages and towns they ran the real risk of being ostracised by their neighbours or being beaten up.

> Nobody who was not actively gay in the early seventies can have any idea how horrible it was, especially for a teenager. At least men over twenty-one could legally have sex. They might be mocked by their workmates and cut off from their families, but at least they had that consolation. Even that was denied to those of us who were still in our teens. We committed a criminal offence every time we kissed! It meant that we were living in a state of fear at the back of our minds. (Anon)

In the 1970s, it was young people who forced an unwilling society to acknowledge that being gay was perfectly acceptable. Gay teenagers saw that they were being sidelined by the sexual revolution which was gaining pace around them. Heterosexual teenagers were enjoying freer lifestyles than their parents could ever have dreamed of;

the contraceptive pill had separated the sexual act from the consequences of pregnancy, and society no longer frowned so sternly upon pre-marital sex. It was perfectly acceptable for a seventeen-year-old boy and girl to go to bed, and the state would even provide them with free contraception if they wished. Gay teenagers felt that they were in some way being left behind. Why should their lives not be granted the same respect as those of heterosexual couples?

> I used to feel bitter that my girlfriend and I could not just tell everybody that we were in love and be accepted as a couple. It wasn't quite as bad for us as it was for gay men. We could hold hands and walk arm-in-arm without anybody saying anything. I had known gay teenage boys be beaten up for showing affection of this sort in public. Even so, we could not be open about our relationship. After the GLF started, some gays and lesbians became more open and my girlfriend and I came out to some friends at university, although not to our parents. That would have been a step too far. (Anon)

Traditional Views of Sex among Teenagers

It is not suggested that all teenagers in the 1970s were engaging in unlimited sex of all types! It is certainly true that by 1980 there had been great changes in the way that things like heterosexual cohabitation and gay relationships were viewed, but not all teenagers subscribed to these new ideas. For many, the old ways of courtship were still going strong. For example, the engagement party was a major event in the lives of many young people, often taking place for boys and girls aged eighteen or nineteen, and even as young as sixteen or seventeen.

A lot of my friends started 'going steady' when they were seventeen or eighteen, which was often a prelude to getting engaged. I would say that the majority of the girls I was at school with and stayed in touch with were engaged by the time they were twenty. Having an engagement ring was something to show off to your friends. It proved that you at least were not going to be left on the shelf. Once you had that ring on your finger, you might let your boyfriend go a bit further. A fiancé could go a lot further than a mere boyfriend! (Pat Howard)

There were advantages for a young couple who were engaged; since there had been a public commitment to marriage, parents might turn a blind eye to pre-marital sex. Engagement parties at that time were something akin to medieval betrothals. It was practically set in stone that the boy and girl would be getting married and so if they anticipated the married state by a few months and slept together, it was not anything like as unaccep-table as it was for a couple who were just 'going out' to have sex.

I didn't sleep with my boyfriend until we were properly engaged. By that, I mean after the party and he had got me a ring and everything. By that stage, it was more or less in the bag, as you might say. I think a lot of us thought, well, what difference does it make? I'll be doing it with him as soon as we're married anyway. (Anon)

The change in habits relating to sex and marriage since the 1970s is quite astonishing. In the late 1960s, for instance, 40 per cent of teenage girls were married by the time they were twenty. In 1970, first marriages in Britain were running at the rate of 340,000 a year. Today, over three quarters of couples cohabit before marrying. In many cases, that cohabitation does not lead to marriage at all.

6

Getting Around

The almost ubiquitous ownership of cars, which has crept imperceptibly up on us over the last forty years, has had a profound impact on the lives of teenagers. The main effect of most parents having cars is that they will drive their teenage children to places, rather than the kids having to make their own way there. This applies to every aspect of teenage life, from getting to school at the age of thirteen to going to university at eighteen.

When I started at the grammar school in 1971, quite a few of us used to cycle to school. We met up and travelled together. A lot of the girls cycled to school then. You don't often see groups of schoolgirls on bikes these days. It gave us an early independence which many kids don't get until they are a few years older. We live near a secondary school and the roads are absolutely clogged up in the mornings with parents dropping their children off in the morning by car. I don't believe that a single pupil arrived at our secondary school in this way and we would have laughed at the very idea. In that way, having bikes and our parents not having cars was a good thing for us. (Mary A. Barker)

I blush to admit that I was still driving my son to school
when he was fourteen. It just seemed quicker and cheaper
than making him get up earlier and get the bus. When I
was his age, in the late seventies, I used to cycle to school
or walk. Cycling is just too dangerous today, with all the
traffic on the roads, and he never seems to walk anywhere.
I suppose that this too is my fault. When he was small I
wouldn't let him walk to school, in case he was run over or
abducted. I was walking to school on my own from the age
of eight or nine. I realise that we have produced a teenager
who never goes anywhere under his own steam, but it just
seemed safer and more convenient. (Maria T. Valentine)

One of the first and most common means of travel used by
teenagers in the 1970s, especially for making long-distance
journeys from city to city, and a method of transport which
has almost vanished completely, was hitchhiking.

My blood runs cold when I remember the risks I took as a
teenager travelling around the country. When I was seventeen I hitched from London to Manchester to see a friend.
I had a couple of hairy moments with men trying it on,
but I managed to extricate myself. I drove my daughter
everywhere when she was that age, just so that I could be
sure that she wasn't taking any chances and would arrive
safely. (Katherine Cassidy)

Hitchhiking, or 'hitching', was once the accepted way for
an older teenager to get from one place to another. If one
lived in Manchester and wanted to attend a concert in
London then the best way of getting there was by rising
early and hitching a lift. Trains were expensive and besides,
what would have been the point? If you were going to be

going to a pop concert, you could probably find better use for your money than spending it on a ticket from British Rail! Sometimes parents would give their kids the money to travel by train or coach, only for the teenager to pocket the money and hitch anyway.

> If I was going to visit my boyfriend in London, my mother would always give me the money for the train, so that I wouldn't hitch. I suppose at the age of seventeen your conscience is not as tender as it is when you are older because I did not think twice about pocketing the money and then hitching up there anyway. If I wanted to do something like that for my own daughter these days, I would buy the tickets online. Not that it is a big thing now; I don't believe any teenagers hitch anywhere these days. (Mary A. Barker)

> We used to hitch everywhere. Even for short distances, a few miles into town. I wouldn't have thought of getting the bus, there was sure to be somebody who would give me a lift. It was the same for longer journeys, going to London, say, which was about 200 miles away. Why on earth would I have paid for a ticket on the train when I could get there for nothing? It wouldn't have made any sense. (Mick Parker)

Approach roads to motorways were good places to pick up a lift and it was not uncommon to find queues of teenagers at such places, each patiently waiting his or her turn. Lay-bys were also good places to wait, although really any road where a driver could stop was acceptable. The convention was that you could hitch on motorways or in rural areas, but that standing in a city hitching was not sensible.

I would not have dreamed of going anywhere by train
or coach. There was only one way to get about and that
was by hitching. Apart from the fact that it was free, it
was exciting. You never knew who would pick you up or
how far they would be able to take you. It was certainly
easier and quicker for girls to get a lift but even so I never
had to wait more than twenty minutes or half an hour for
a ride. Getting people to pick up more than one person
could be tricky. When my girlfriend and I were hitching,
she would stand there waving her thumb and I would stay
out of sight. Then if a car stopped, I would jump out and
we would both climb in. Some drivers were annoyed by
this, but nobody ever chucked us out after having this trick
played on them. (Martin O'Connell)

Some of these hitchhikers were not going anywhere in
particular, just travelling round as a form of holiday.
Mind, one did not call it a 'holiday', it was being 'on
the road', as though you were some latter day Jack
Kerouac. If you knew where you were going and wanted
a lift all the way there, then you might print the name
of the city on a piece of cardboard and hold it up. This
would avoid having to take a succession of short lifts
and might, if you were lucky, get you a lift all the way to
your destination.

Being 'on the road' made us feel as though we were the
heroes of some beat novel. I used to go to festivals and so
on, always hitching. It was part of the whole thing in the
seventies, hitching from place to place. I haven't seen anybody hitching for years now. I suppose that teenagers have
more money and, possibly, more sense than they did when I
was young. (Geoffrey C. Feldman)

As a rule, it was less than likely that one would get a lift all the way to where you were going. Travelling from London to Exeter might entail six rides, each taking you in the right direction. One might take you to Reading, the next to Salisbury and so on. Even so, hitching was a surprisingly fast means of travel; it was unusual to have to wait more than ten or fifteen minutes for a ride.

> I have not seen any young person hitching for about ten years or so. It is very funny and I can't think what the explanation can be. When I was at university that was just how you got around. I was at Exeter, but lived a little way out of town. I would always hitch the five miles or so to the university in the morning and never had to wait long for a lift. People seemed to take it for granted that teenagers would travel like this and many drivers would stop. A lot of them were middle-aged parents themselves and so I suppose it was viewed as a quid pro quo; today they picked up somebody else's son or daughter and tomorrow, somebody would do the same for their children. (Katherine Cassidy)

Single girls found it easiest of all to get rides, partly because drivers worried about their safety, perhaps remembering their own daughters. Some of course had baser motives and while rapes were very rare it was not uncommon for a man to try it on with a teenage girl whom he had picked up in this way. It was this fear which caused so many parents to place a blanket ban on the custom of hitchhiking. Such bans were all too often ignored by the teenage girls themselves.

> We weren't on the phone and neither were some of my friends. This meant that we could claim to be staying

overnight there and, short of coming round in person, there was no way my parents could know I wasn't. I pulled this stroke one weekend, I must have been seventeen, it was the mid-seventies, and the two of us hitched off to the free festival at Windsor. Two girls – one sixteen and the other seventeen – jumping into cars with complete strangers; my parents would have gone mad had they known, but they never found out. (Mary A. Barker)

I never told my mother and father that I hitched all over the place. There was a mythology about girls hitchhiking, which was to the effect that they would end up being raped or strangled by some maniac. I never heard of anything of the sort ever happening to anybody I knew. Come to that, I don't even remember seeing any cases like that in the news-papers. It was just that that was what our parents thought would be likely to happen. (Esther M. Hannigan)

This was a time when a student heading off to university could pack all that they might need for the term into a single suitcase or backpack, which meant that hitching was a quite practical proposition for travelling to and from university. Anybody who has a child at university today will know that even a car is barely sufficient to transport their son or daughter and all their belongings for the term. A removal van would be better in many cases.

When I moved to London in 1977 at the age of eighteen, I packed a backpack and hitched there and established myself in a bedsit. My parents had no part in the business at all. When my own son moved into his first place, when he went to university last year, we had to make two journeys in the car. Laptops, a television, DVD player and God alone

knows what else. He would have been hard-pressed to
hitch with all that lot. (Terry Barlow)

Drivers today will know that one simply never sees young
hitchhikers hanging around near motorways any more.
Even if one was seen, how many drivers today would feel
comfortable to pick up an unknown person in this way?

> It is one of those images from the seventies which linger on
> in my mind. Standing by the side of the road while it was
> raining and there was hardly any traffic about, trying to get
> a lift. If you were not careful, you could end up romanticis-
> ing the whole hitching business and thinking that it all took
> place on gloriously hot August days, when the lifts came
> thick and fast every five minutes. It wasn't always like that
> of course and there were plenty of times that I would rather
> have got a bus or train than been standing in the open get-
> ting soaking wet. (K.A. Silverstone)

> I had one or two hairy moments when hitching, but noth-
> ing out of the ordinary. One guy pulled over and tried to
> start kissing me. I swore at him and just got out of the
> car. Another time, a man began talking suggestively and
> I asked him to stop, which he did. This time it was him
> that swore at me; accusing me of leading him on. I don't
> think that either of these incidents harmed me and they
> certainly taught me how to stand up for myself. (Maria
> T. Valentine)

It is interesting to speculate about just what brought about
the end of hitchhiking in this country. There is no doubt at
all that a few years ago it was still going strong, but then
seemed to end abruptly.

The heyday of hitching was definitely the seventies. It was quite simply how teenagers got from place to place. You still saw kids hitching in the eighties, but by the nineties it was certainly on the way out as an accepted mode of transport. It must be ten years since I saw any young person standing hopefully by the side of the road. Perhaps the fact that most people have cars has something to do with it. After all, if your daughter is going off to university a hundred miles away, you would be expected today to drive her there. There is no incentive for young people to hitchhike. Some of it might be the 'Stranger Danger' campaign to which they have all been exposed at school. (Gillian V. Pettitt)

Whatever the explanation, hitching – like so many other features of teenage life in the 1970s – seems to have all but vanished from the British scene. Whether it has gone for good is another matter. Perhaps, if there is a fierce enough recession and money becomes much shorter, young people will once again take to the road.

Cars

In 1970, there were 15 million cars on the road in this country. Today, that figure has more than doubled. As the decade began, it was still common to see groups of teenagers cycling to school together. Today, such a sight is practically unknown. If a teenager wished to travel across town or to or from an evening activity, parents will almost always offer lifts.

My parents didn't have a car so they couldn't have given me a lift anyway. Even if they had though, I doubt if they would have been driving me everywhere. In the 1970s, by the time you were teenager you were more or less expected to be getting a bit more independent. The lack of cars helped that, teenagers had to get where they were going under their own steam and this involved making decisions and learning to look after themselves. (Martin O'Connell)

Forty years ago, it was seen as perfectly normal that a bunch of teenagers leaving a youth club should walk home together, chatting and laughing as they went. They might stop en route and sit on walls for a time. In the 1970s, a bunch of young teenagers coming home from a youth club would not have raised any eyebrows. Today, such gatherings of young people have become a little less common and are viewed with suspicion, seen as 'gangs' who are, perhaps, about to engage in 'anti-social behaviour'.

I don't recall anybody being worried about me and my mates when we were walking about in the evening. We used to hang about the centre of town, sitting on walls, smoking and chatting. I suppose that the worst we might actually do was whistle at some pretty girl. The local bobby used to pass by and stop and chat to us. There was no animosity and he certainly didn't see us as a problem to be dealt with. When it got dark, we would drift home in ones and twos. In our local area last year, because teenagers were hanging round the car park of the local supermarket, the police obtained an order covering all the nearby streets, which banned teenagers from being there after nine o'clock in the evening. Completely bonkers – I have passed those kids and they were doing exactly what we used to do forty years ago, just sitting and chatting. People complained about them, though, and claimed that they felt intimidated. (Paul Clarke)

I left school in 1977 and at that time it was very common
to see groups of teenagers just hanging around and doing
nothing much in particular. I know, because I was one of
them. In the summer we used to sit on the grass near the
town centre, just relaxing and talking. I still live in the same
town and now have a fifteen-year-old daughter. Last year
she was really worried because she had seen a sign fixed to
a lamp post by the police, saying that an anti-social behaviour order had been granted to the police and that young
people under the age of sixteen should not be using certain
streets in the evening. Since my daughter's violin teacher
lived in one of the streets, she was put in the ludicrous position of having to break the law to come home from her
music lesson. (Maria T. Valentine)

In the 1970s, meeting your friends and then wandering
round doing nothing much except chatting and perhaps
listening to a transistor radio was a free way of spending
time. Going to and from places like a church youth club
was part of the socialising which took place. No adult
would be at all concerned at the sight of a bunch of teenagers walking towards them; why would they? This is not to
say that funny remarks might not be called out at passers-
by or that the odd bit of mischief would not occur, but it
was not seen as any sort of problem.

We didn't have as much money when I was a teenager as the
kids today seem to have. There was no question of my mother
chucking me £10 or £20 to go to the cinema or McDonald's.
A natural consequence was that if you did not want to stop
in the house with your mum and dad every evening and, let's
face it, what teenager does, then you would be roaming the
streets with your friends a lot. (Gillian V. Pettitt)

From the time I was fourteen or fifteen, I was regularly out
in the evenings without my parents being able to contact
me or having much idea where I was. I would say, 'I'm
going round Mike's house,' and then I would be off. This
was 1975/76, and I was careful to use the names of friends
whose parents weren't on the telephone. I might actually go
to Mike's house, of course, but then we would be out and
about with our mates. We walked everywhere and often did
nothing more than sit around the park talking. I had to get
where I was going under my own steam and home again. I
can't imagine what it would have taken for me to ring my
parents while I was out. It was almost a rite of passage,
being out of contact with your parents; it was like training
for adult life. (Paul Clarke)

Forty years ago, a teenager wanting to get home after
losing or more likely spending all their money, would have
little choice but to work out for themselves how to do so.
The chances were that their parents were not on the telephone and even if they could get in touch with them, they
would probably not be able to drive over and collect them
in the car. This forced the young person to think for themselves and devise a way out of their problem. Sometimes,
this would involve begging the fare money from strangers,
on other occasions it could mean hitching a lift or even
walking home.

I can't remember the precise circumstances that led to it,
but when I was fifteen I managed to get myself stranded
alone in central London without a single penny. If I had
had enough money for a platform ticket, then I could have
got onto the tube and bluffed my way through the ticket
barrier at the other end. As it was, I tried begging money

from passers-by and when that didn't work I asked the
ticket collector to let me through and promised to pay at
the other end. When I got to Ealing, I just legged it through
the barrier. My parents weren't on the phone, so there was
no way of calling them for help. I think that experiences
like this helped me to become self-sufficient and find ways
of coping. My own son would probably just text me and
ask to be picked up in the car. (David Ford)

Bicycles

The bicycle was the most common way of getting from
A to B among teenagers during the 1970s. Of course,
the bicycle was more than merely a means of transport.
It could also be a status symbol, just as the most up-to-
date model of car is for many adults today. Your bike told
people a lot about you. However, it must be borne in mind
that at this time many adults still rode bikes as well, as it
was the cheapest way of getting to work in the morning.

My dad used to cycle to work because it was quick and
cheap. He couldn't afford a car and so he used a bike. I got
my first bike when I was twelve and also, more or less as a
matter of routine, found myself cycling everywhere. I cycled
to school, to visit friends and also as a hobby, I would go
into the countryside on the bike. Because far fewer people
had cars at that time, the bicycle was accepted as the main
means of transport in many families. (Geoffrey C. Feldman)

Some bicycles had more style than others. Having a bike with
the old-fashioned 'sit up and beg' handlebars was not cool
and most young people wanted to have drop-handlebars.

We were not very well off and I inherited my dad's bike when he finally bought a car. It was a very old-fashioned thing, not some sleek model with drop-handlebars or anything like that; just a standard bicycle. This was when I was fourteen or fifteen and all my friends either had choppers or racing bikes. Here was I with a 1950s-style bicycle such as you might expect to see the vicar riding. The shame of it! (Martin O'Connell)

Choppers

Choppers were customised motorbikes which originated in America during the 1960s. They were designed with a large back wheel, padded seat with backrest, loads of chrome and so on. In the late 1960s, somebody had the idea of producing a version of this kind of motorbike for teenagers. The only difference was that these would not be customised and they would not be motorbikes. The result was a 1970s icon; the chopper.

The chopper! I can still remember how important it was to me to have a chopper rather than an ordinary bike. A group of us all had choppers and we felt that we were like Hell's Angels. The footrest made it possible for you to leave the thing leaning at an angle, just like the motorbikes in *Easy Rider*. Then there was the gear handle. The ordinary Sturmey-Archer gears had a titchy little switch which was stuck on the handlebars. With the chopper though, you had a gearstick, just like the one in a car. It was just so different from any other bike. (Terry Barlow)

The chopper looked a bit like the bike that Peter Fonda rode in *Easy Rider*. Well, it was close enough to seem

convincing to teenage boys. Everything about this bicycle
was new and exciting; it was completely different from the
traditional bicycle that everybody else had. It had a high-
back seat, long enough to seat two so that you could give
your friends rides, a gear change knob, like the one in a
car instead of the fiddly little gear change box on the handlebars of ordinary bikes, and even the kickstand let the
bike stand at a jaunty angle; giving it another superficial
resemblance to a motorbike rather than a pedal cycle.

> I begged and pleaded with my parents for a chopper. It
> had only come out the previous year, so I suppose this
> must have been 1971, when I was fifteen. They just looked
> so cool compared with my dad's old bike that he let me
> use sometimes. There was something really exotic about
> them, which ordinary bikes just didn't have. They were not
> functional; for example, they were very wobbly and if you
> leaned back too far you could find yourself unexpectedly
> doing a wheelie, but when they were parked they sat there
> at an angle, just like *Easy Rider*. (David Ford)

When the chopper went on sale in the UK in 1970, it
became the must-have item for every young teenage boy.
There were one or two disadvantages, but nothing to
bother the teenagers themselves. For parents, the price
was a big problem. The standard model chopper was £32,
which works out at nearly £500 in modern terms. This was
an astronomical sum to spend on a bike. The deluxe version was almost twice as expensive, retailing for £55.

> I got a chopper for my fourteenth birthday in 1971. It was
> an unbelievable surprise, as they were so expensive that I
> never really thought that my parents would be able to get

me one. What I did not know at the time, and did not learn until years later, was that my father had bought it on hire purchase. This meant that he was still paying for it two years later, long after the novelty had worn off and I had lost interest in it, as I was almost sixteen. (Geoffrey C. Feldman)

The real problem with the chopper, as anybody who was riding one at the time will know only too well, was that it was horribly unstable and downright dangerous to ride. The small front wheel, combined with the far-back seat, made one liable to perform wheelies unexpectedly while cycling along the road. This was especially likely if the long seat had tempted you to give your mate a ride at the same time. Put bluntly, the chopper was badly designed from a safety point of view. It wobbled alarmingly at almost any speed and was famously tricky to steer. Those high chrome handlebars might look cool, but they made turning corners an absolute nightmare!

Those of us with choppers knew perfectly well that they weren't as easy to ride as ordinary bikes. There was a kind of conspiracy of silence amongst chopper owners, whereby we would discuss their shortcomings between ourselves but not admit to anybody else that they were buggers to ride. Giving a friend a ride on your crossbar on a normal bike actually made the thing more stable, by increasing the weight between the wheels. With the long seat on the chopper and that jutting up gear change handle, you gave people rides on the back of the seat. This shifted the balance to the rear wheel and if you weren't careful, the front wheel would leave the ground. Even without that though, they were harder to steer than most bikes, even without twisting the handlebars back to front as some of us did. (Terry Barlow)

The press inveighed against what was described as a dangerous new novelty and this led to the release of the Mk II chopper in 1972, a supposedly safer and more stable model. Throughout the whole of the 1970s, the chopper reigned supreme, rescuing bike-making company Raleigh from insolvency. The craze faded a little as enthusiasm grew for BMX bikes and production of the chopper stopped in 1981.

> The chopper was one of those things which really only lasted during the seventies. It was tremendously cool and fashionable in 1972 and then, less than a decade later, demand had fallen to almost nothing and the company stopped making them. The chopper is one of those visual images which belong to that period so completely. If you were a teenager and still had an ordinary bike by 1975, then you really were a bit of a loser (unless your bike was some fantastic racing model with twelve speed gears, drop-handlebars and a water bottle clipped to the crossbar, that is). (David Ford)

The chopper is the perfect example of a 1970s fad which began in 1970 and ended almost precisely ten years later at the end of the decade. Platform shoes and 8 Track Stereos fall into the same category. They are all things which are instantly recognisable as being of that time and were, moreover, all seen to be ultra-modern at the time. Within a few years of the 1970s ending, all these things had a hopelessly old-fashioned look about them.

> My teenage years spanned both the late seventies and early eighties. I was thirteen in 1975 and turned twenty at the end of 1981. What I do have is a very vivid memory of the sudden end of the seventies, in terms of those things which

became abruptly out of fashion. Platform shoes had been popular since 1970 or 1971 and then in 1979, without any warning, they could no longer be worn. The same thing happened with the chopper. They were the very thing to have if you were a young teenage boy in the late seventies and then, again with no warning, they were replaced with BMX bikes and nobody wanted to be seen on a chopper. It was almost as though everybody had had enough of the seventies and decided collectively to ditch some of its most potent symbols. (Maria T. Valentine)

Buses and Trains

Hitching was fine for moving from city to city and a bike was handy for getting around in your immediate neighbourhood, but for travelling across a city, one sometimes had to use public transport. Almost every teenager knew well enough how to travel around in this way for either nothing or at least a minimal outlay. It is very hard today to fiddle one's fares, what with the electronic barriers at stations and one-man buses.

My friends and I never paid fares if we could possibly avoid it. It was so much easier then than it is now. I left school in 1978 and in those days all the ticket barriers on the tube consisted of a human ticket collector. There were a million ways of getting past on your way out of the station if you didn't have a ticket. The most obvious was to approach the fellow at a casual saunter and then, suddenly and unexpectedly, break into a sprint. By the time he realised what was happening, you would be out of the station and halfway down the road. Another tactic was to claim that you had

lost your ticket and offer your name and address; obviously
not the correct one. The old Routemasters were great for
getting round for nothing. You could jump on a bus at the
lights and then by the time the conductor came to you, you
could discover that you had a hole in your pocket and your
money had fallen out of it. Even if he chucked you off the
bus – and not all would – with a little luck you would be a
mile or so further down the road in the direction you were
heading by then. (Paul Clarke)

In 1970, city buses had both a driver and a conductor. One
simply hopped on at the platform at the back, which was
completely open. This meant that one could get on and off
at traffic lights or if the bus just happened to be moving
slowly in traffic. If the conductor was upstairs, then it was
possible to nip on and sit down, trying to look as though
you had already paid your fare. This could be done by staring out of the window and ignoring the conductor's cry of
'Any more fares?'

It was always worth giving it a go and trying to avoid paying
on the bus. I found that pretending to be utterly absorbed
in a book sometimes worked, as did staring intently and
thoughtfully out of the window. The conductors couldn't
keep track of everybody who had paid their fares and there
was always a good chance of getting away with it. Some
conductors, though, didn't like or trust teenagers and even
if you had paid your fare, they would demand to see the
ticket just to be on the safe side, to make sure that no young
person was putting one over them. These days, such games
are impossible. If a teenager tries to slip past the driver without paying his fare, the man will usually just turn off the
engine and radio to his headquarters. (Christopher Walker)

The battle of wits between the conductor and the teenager determined to travel on his bus for nothing was a time-honoured ritual. Many conductors didn't care; others made certain never to let any young scamp put one over them. If challenged, one claimed to have paid the fare and implied that the conductor must be a forgetful sort of man if he couldn't remember selling you a ticket. Of course, the crunch came when he demanded to see the alleged ticket. All these exchanges and delays of course took you further along the road and when, as sometimes happened, you were thrown off the bus, then at least you had travelled a mile or so, rather than having to walk.

> It was practically an obligation among the set to whom I belonged that we would not offer our fares to the bus conductor. The usual routine was that when he passed, passengers would hold up their money and state their destination. We would have scorned to do this. It was only a trifling sum, but better in your pocket than the bank account of London Transport. It was a sad day in the mid-seventies when they started bringing in one-conductor-only buses. The first route I saw them on was the 169, running from Barking to Fulwell Cross. Those buses used to crawl along Ilford Lane and there were plenty of handy places to hop on when the conductor was upstairs. (Anon)

These games were, in the main, good-natured and the teenagers knew perfectly well that they were trying it on and when detected would resign themselves to leaving the bus quietly. After all, there would be another one along soon and the same process could be repeated, with luck, until you reached your destination. The introduction of one-man buses in the 1970s ended these tricks. From then on, one could not simply jump on a slow moving bus while the conductor was upstairs; it was impossible to get on a bus at all except when it was at a stop and then one had to walk past the driver collecting fares.

In the 1970s, instead of electronic barriers at railways and tube stations, there was a ticket collector. His attention might be distracted as one tried to enter or leave the station, and on occasion it was possible to slip through with a crowd of people and evade notice in that way or, when all else failed, just dart through without warning and run for it. Few ticket collectors had the energy to give chase to an agile fifteen year old.

Teenage heart-throb: David Cassidy in 1974. (Courtesy of Allan Warren)

The future of teenage communication – the push button Trimphone. (Courtesy of Diamond Magma)

The chopper bicycle, a must-have for teenagers in the 1970s.

Asian youths confront the police in Brick Lane, 1978. (Courtesy of Alan Denney)

Student protest at the London School of Economics, 1979. (Courtesy of the LSE Library)

Teenagers often turned out for marches and demonstrations, such as this National Front march in the 1970s. (Courtesy of Whiteflight)

A joint of cannabis.

Elton John as the Pinball Wizard – an archetype of the 1970s. (Courtesy of Ryan Junell)

The mohican - a
punk haircut.
(Courtesy of
wetwebwork)

Looking
for trouble?
Skinheads
on a day out.
(Courtesy of
Michele Ahin)

Peace man: a hippie
teenager. (Courtesy
of Joyradest)

Striking a pose: flares and long hair were all the rage for teenage boys in the 1970s. (Courtesy of Jeremy Brunger)

An example of 1970s male fashion: no tie in sight! (Courtesy of Stephen Briancourt)

A precious commodity: a record player from the 1970s.

A selection of popular albums released in the 1970s. Records were prized possessions.

A day trip in the car. (Courtesy of Jeremy Brunger)

A trip to the seaside in the Ford Capri in the 1970s. (Courtesy of Jeremy Brunger)

An example of fashion in the 1970s. (Courtesy of Jeremy Brunger)

Point and click: a Kodak Instamatic camera. (Courtesy of Dirk Meye)

A Silver Jubilee street party, February 1977.

7

Politics

In the 1970s it was commonplace to hear of teenagers protesting against one cause of another. Nowadays, one seldom hears of students marching on behalf of the human rights violations in some country or the other. However, forty years ago things were very different.

> It may just be because I am getting old, but I very strongly have the impression that students in the seventies used to care more about what was going on in the world; there wasn't a single person in my class at college who didn't know about Barclays Bank and their connection with South Africa. We used to call it 'Barclays Blood Bank' and no student would have dreamed of having an account with them. (Christopher Walker)

Teenagers in the 1970s would have viewed protests as a form of something to do, when there was often very little else to do. Marches and demonstrations could be thought of as a free form of entertainment, as they were often associated with music and free festivals.

I remember the first Rock Against Racism festival in 1978. A whole bunch of us met for the rally in Trafalgar Square and then marched all the way to Victoria Park. There were some fantastic bands there and we met a great bunch of people. It combined a completely free day's entertainment with good music, with the feeling that we were taking part in something worthwhile that might help to change society. (Anon)

From spring to autumn my friends and I were doing outdoor stuff on as many weekends as we could. Sometimes it was festivals and concerts, other times it was marches. There was a great sense of camaraderie on demonstrations and it used to get me out of the house for the day. Sometimes we would travel to some provincial town where a factory was making parts for a weapons system or to somewhere a South African sports team was playing. It was a way of life for many students at that time. (Christopher Walker)

Another reason why so many more teenagers in the 1970s were politically active was that this was a decade of turmoil in Britain, during the course of which it was practically impossible to forget about politics. Throughout the decade it was not really possible for anybody in this country to ignore politics.

I was thirteen in 1972 and the nature of politics was brought home to me very forcefully that year by the miners, who went on strike. This led to my grandfather telling me that they had not been on strike since 1926. More to the point, there were power cuts as the fuel stocks diminished. In our area, the electricity was off for nine hours a day, which meant living by candlelight and oil lamp with no television or anything. This naturally made us talk about the Heath government and what was going on. Our family weren't very political, but when you suddenly find yourself having to live by candlelight as though you are back in Victorian times, it does rather make you ask questions about why it is happening. (Terry Barlow)

The three-day week which Heath first imposed in 1972 was when I came to realise that politics is not some sort of airy fairy abstraction, but something which affects ordinary people. My father was working in a factory at the time and we suddenly found that his pay had dropped by 40 per cent, because the factory went on short time during the miners' strike that year. I had turned eighteen the year before and had not really thought about who I was going to vote for. The voting age had only recently been reduced from twenty-one to eighteen and so I knew that at the next election I would be able to vote. The events of the early seventies provided teenagers with a primer of just why politics mattered. (K.A. Silverstone)

Experiencing large-scale power cuts made ordinary teenagers aware of the political situation in their country in a way that no number of party political broadcasts or leading articles in the newspapers could do. Perhaps only a minority of young people were politically active to the extent that they would go on demonstrations, but every single teenager in the country knew about it when the power went off and they could not see *Top of the Pops* that night!

When the government declared a state of emergency in February 1972, even the people that I used to hang round the record shop with started talking about politics. Some of them had fathers who were now working a three-day week and were getting hard up. That, combined with the daily

power cuts, made politics a bit more important than just
what you saw on the news. (Theresa O. Littlestone)

If the 1972 miners' strike brought home to teenagers just
what politics could mean to them and their families, the
following year came as an even greater shock. For several
years, the troubles in Northern Ireland had been turning
uglier. For most young people in Britain though, this was
no more than another aspect of politics which had no
direct bearing upon their lives. That was until 1973, when
bombs began exploding in English cities.

I can't tell you what a shock it was to see scenes of devasta-
tion in London caused by bombs in the spring of 1973. My
parents remembered the Blitz of the Second World War, but
I grew up in the fifties and sixties, which were completely
peaceful in England. To see on the television shattered
vehicles and injured people and to realise that an attack had
taken place only a few miles from where I was living was
shocking. I suppose that most eighteen year olds in London
at that time, like me, had never taken much of an interest in
Irish politics, but once the IRA campaign started, I have to
admit that I began reading the newspapers more to try and
understand why it was happening. (Mick Parker)

Political dispute in Britain came to a climax in November
1974, when twenty-one people were killed in two explo-
sions in crowded pubs.

I remember that some pubs were searching people's bags
as they came in. Clubs in London had sandbags piled up in
front of the windows. There was definitely an air of crisis.
This was in very sharp contrast to the way things had been

when I was at school in the late sixties. There had been no
such thing as political violence then and it was possible to
ignore politics. You couldn't ignore the 1974 miners' strike
and the IRA though. (Pat Howard)

Power cuts, terrorist attacks, food shortages, galloping
inflation and two General Elections in one year; it was
pretty hard to ignore politics if you were living in Britain in
1974. Teenagers, just like everybody else, took sides in the
various strikes and disputes.

I was at secondary school in 1972 and was still there in 1974.
We all talked about the power cuts and the three-day week.
The novelty of spending the evening with your parents, the
house lit only by candles and oil lamps, was such that we
were bound to discuss it the next day at school. Some were
on the miners' side and others thought that Heath was right
to stand up to them. Everybody had an opinion though. The
same thing happened when the IRA started bombing the
mainland in 1973. There was a lot of anger about that, but it
definitely meant that teenagers at school were debating politics seriously during their lunch hour, a thing which I would
be surprised to hear happens these days. (Paul Clarke)

The 1950s and '60s had been particularly quiet and safe
decades. Politics had been a gentle business and for most
teenagers, their memories of political activity at this time
entailed no more than their parents voting in 1964 or 1966
for either Harold Wilson or Edward Heath. Most teenagers then were not all that bothered about politics; it was the
sort of thing that the older generation worried about. Of
course, a few belonged to CND and so on, but by and large
young people found that politics did not impinge all that

much on their own lives. The 1970s changed all that with a vengeance. From 1970 onwards, politics meant strikes, shortages, power cuts, terrorism, riots and disorder, and it was something teenagers could no longer ignore.

> I suppose that like many who were teenagers during the seventies, I found that it was not possible just to coast along without thinking about things like Northern Ireland or inflation or the standard of living of miners in South Wales. If you were without electricity for eight hours, you wanted to know why. The papers showed pictures of miners' homes in some parts of Britain and this was shocking to a teenager living in a comfortable house in the Home Counties. It forced me to think about the inequalities that existed in society. In the same way, one could no longer pretend that Ulster was a private quarrel between two sets of excitable Irishmen; not when people were being killed by explosions in Guildford, as happened in October 1974. I don't think that it is an exaggeration to say that the seventies made an entire generation of teenagers politically aware. (Mary A. Barker)

As the decade progressed, the feeling that politics were something which did actually concern young people became stronger. In 1976, the Notting Hill Carnival exploded in ferocious rioting, thus drawing attention to the grievances of ethnic minority teenagers living in the capital. Just like the terrorist attacks which had started a few years earlier, rioting was not something one associated with England. Further riots took place in Lewisham and Southall. It was starting to look as though the very fabric of society was cracking. By 1978, the Winter of Discontent was here and the regular strikes had increased until they had plainly got out of hand. Mounds of rubbish built up in gardens and parks, unemployment was at a peak; it looked as though Britain was falling to pieces.

> My main memory of the seventies is that of a continuous crisis, as though we were lurching from one near-disaster to the next. Bombs, riots, strikes, inflation, unemployment; you really didn't know what to expect next. Like all teen-agers then I had grown up in a country which was stable and orderly, a dull place where nothing much seemed to happen. Now, everything was changing and Britain sud-denly appeared to be a dangerous and unstable place to be living. Emigration increased and there was even talk of the possibility of a military coup. A few years earlier groups of teenagers in the pub would have been talking about nothing more important than football, now they were discussing the IRA or the grievances of the miners. (Katherine Cassidy)

On a less dramatic note, in 1974 it was still something of a novelty for teenagers to vote at the General Election. Although they had been able to vote since 1970, it was still an unusual sight to see youngsters in school uniform going into the polling booths on their way to school.

Demonstrations

In 1970, the war in Vietnam was in full swing and there were regular demonstrations in London to protest against the American bombing. The average age on these marches was probably around nineteen or twenty. This was a cause that teenagers cared about. Similarly, the CND marches every Easter were events which attracted huge numbers of teenagers. Typically, they culminated in street theatre, fes-tivals and pop concerts. One in 1970, although essentially political, included a pop concert at the Roundhouse and a festival in Victoria Park in East London.

> Most weeks in the early seventies, *Time Out* mentioned protest marches and demonstrations which would be taking place. Attending such events became quite a hobby of the college students with whom I hung around; one week it might be Vietnam, another Ban the Bomb or perhaps Rhodesia. You would see the same people on these demos, just the placards and banners were different. (Polly Reynolds)

Photographs of protests from the time show that the majority of participants were teenagers. Just as the more right-wing type of young person tended to become embroiled in violent confrontations at football matches, so the left-wing ones used to attend demonstrations and hurl abuse, even at the police.

> Going on marches was a social activity as much as anything else. You met up with friends there and saw the same people on all sorts of different causes. There was an air of excitement about demonstrations, because we were showing the straights – ordinary dull people – what we believed in. It was also good fun to bate the police and see how far we could push them before they would react and get nasty. I remember one march, calling for the pedestrianisation of Oxford Street, which was held on the last Saturday before Christmas in 1971. We just crossed and re-crossed the roads around Selfridges, holding up the traffic until the police decided to arrest us all. I was seventeen at the time and this was the first time that I had been arrested. Quite an experience; it made us feel like political prisoners when we were locked in the cells at Holborn police station! (Christopher Walker)

As the decade progressed, violence between teenagers and young people at protests increased; this was particularly so in demonstrations aimed at the National Front. In 1976, the first serious riot in England of the twentieth century took place following disorder at the Notting Hill Carnival. This was followed in 1977 by rioting in the south London district of Lewisham, which, like Notting Hill, was an area with a high concentration of ethnic minorities.

> I was at the Notting Hill Carnival in 1976 and also went to Lewisham the following year to protest against the National Front. One of the things which I noticed on both occasions was that a lot of the young people there had come only to cause trouble and attack the police. There might have been legitimate grievances, but many of the crowd were behaving like football hooligans. (Christopher Walker)

Racist attacks on Black and Asian people became common during the 1970s, fuelled and incited by the National Front. Although their political message of halting immigration and expelling ethnic minorities already living in the UK was repugnant to many, some teenagers took to it. As a reaction to this, Rock Against Racism was founded in 1976 and organised some big concerts, which they combine with political protests against racism.

The 1970s were a time of confrontation and conflict in this country. The miners' strike, which brought down the Heath government; the Winter of Discontent; clashes on the streets between the National Front and left-wing students; these became the defining images of the times. It was perhaps inevitable that the music which teenagers were listening to should have reflected aspects of what seemed, to many, to be a continuing crisis throughout much of the decade.

In 1978, a huge free concert was held at Victoria Park in east London. It had been organised by Rock Against Racism and it was the culmination of a 100,000-strong march by young people from Trafalgar Square to Hackney. Among the bands playing at this event were The Clash, The Buzzcocks and the Tom Robinson Band. A few months later, Rock Against Racism organised another concert in south London, where Elvis Costello performed.

It is difficult to say whether events of this sort were pop festivals or political protests; a bit of both really. Those attending them were, without doubt, concerned about the increasing racism which they saw in this country, but were also glad of the opportunity to attend a free concert featuring some top names from the music scene.

8

Television

During the 1970s, television played a pretty big part in the lives of most teenagers, for several reasons. For one thing, we have seen that there were not nearly as many distractions available to young people who were staying indoors forty years ago as is the case today. No mobile phones to stare at, no games consoles, Internet, computers, DVDs and all the rest of the paraphernalia of modern youth.

> In retrospect, my evenings at home when I was a teenager were like some sort of experiment in sensory deprivation. There was absolutely nothing to do for much of the time. The only entertainment was of course provided by the television. Because there was only one television, this meant that everybody had to sit in the same room, more or less side by side to watch it. There were only three channels all through my teenage years; Channel 4 didn't start broadcasting until 1982. A consequence of this was that watching television was a more social event. (Chris Arthur)

With only three channels and no video recorders, watching a film on television meant that teenagers would have to sit down with everybody else at the same time. Apart from Open University programmes on BBC 2, there was little or no daytime television and programmes finished at around midnight. This all meant that teenagers from that time will generally share a common cultural heritage; they almost all watched the same programmes. It is a racing certainty, for instance, that anybody now aged between forty-five and sixty will have watched *The Generation Game* with Bruce Forsyth during the 1970s.

> *The Generation Game*! It became something of a catch-phrase in our house, 'Didn't he do well!' This was the perfect family entertainment, because it featured families of course. There was nothing smutty, nothing that you would not be comfortable watching with your granny or your little sister. It was just good fun. Everybody watched it; I can't imagine a teenager who did not see it on Saturdays. There is nothing comparable these days in the way of television programmes. My kids watch stuff on catch-up TV or YouTube, my husband and I watch DVDs of films we like and the children watch what they enjoy. I can't remember when we last sat down as a family, all watching the same film or television programme. Perhaps we wouldn't have done so in the seventies if we had have had more than one TV in the house or a video recorder. We didn't though and so we all shared the same experience of mass entertainment. (Gillian V. Pettitt)

So what were teenagers watching in the 1970s? Everybody, young and old, tuned into comedy programmes like *Steptoe & Son*, *On the Buses* and *Please Sir!* These were national institutions and you would have to go a long way

to find a teenager who didn't know what day they were on
or who did not watch them with their parents.

> There was something reassuring about sitting down as
> a family and laughing at something like *Steptoe & Son*.
> It provided some common ground between me and my
> parents. We didn't seem to have much in common as I
> grew older, until by the time I was nineteen or twenty I
> could hardly think of anything that my parents and I felt
> the same about. Throughout those years though, we still
> carried on watching things like the *Benny Hill Show* and
> *Morecombe and Wise*. Watching telly together was a kind
> of glue, which held us together. The very act of chortling
> together at Benny Hill's antics told us that we did have
> something in common. (Mary A. Barker)

Until the middle of the twentieth century, the focal point
in the living room of most homes was the fireplace. This
was where people clustered round and all the furniture
was angled to point in that direction. During the 1950s
and '60s, the focal point gradually shifted from the
hearth to the television set. By the 1970s, this movement
was complete.

> There was something comforting about going into the room
> with the television. I used to row with my parents a bit, but
> you couldn't row if you weren't talking! In our house, you
> would hear the characters from *Last of the Summer Wine*
> talking more than we did. You might think that we would
> argue over what to watch, but that very rarely happened. If
> *Opportunity Knocks* or Some *Mothers Do 'Ave 'Em* was
> on, why would you not want to watch it? Television was
> the one thing we all had in common. (Sarah P. Moran)

One of the most popular television programmes of the 1970s, *Jim'll Fix It*, was first broadcast in the summer of 1975 and it became a firm favourite with teenagers and their parents, as well as younger children. It was aired at teatime on Saturdays and was one of the very first 'reality TV' shows.

> There was very little to do at quarter to six on a Saturday afternoon during the mid-seventies. No computers or mobiles, and with the majority of homes without a telephone, the television was the centre of attention for the whole family. Of course there were some programmes that as a teenager you would not want to sit down and watch with your mum and dad; *Come Dancing* or the *Black and White Minstrels Show*, for example. There were others though, like the *Generation Game* and *Jim'll Fix It* that were perfect entertainment for the whole family. The young people who sent in their requests were often teenagers themselves and when they weren't, they were younger children who reminded you of your own young brother or sister. Although as teenagers we might have mocked the thing, it was still unmissable. (Mary A. Barker)

As it is now, occasionally an item of clothing, a singer, or a catchphrase would appear form nowhere and before you knew it, everybody was gripped by it. *Monty Python* was a bit like that. It was originally released in October 1969, but was on late and not many people knew of it. Then suddenly, you just had to watch it; people were doing the sketches at college and quoting from it. I doubt that there was a teenager in the country who was not a fan of the show by the end of 1970.

Few teenagers would watch anything on BBC 2 and so really there were only two television channels being watched by young people on a regular basis. Combine this with the fact that there was little other form of amusement in the home at that time and it is easy to see why popular television programmes became a common bond between teenagers. When that choice is limited to only two channels and there is nothing else to do on a dark winter's evening, it is easy to see why practically anybody who is now fifty or sixty will remember such programmes as *Dr Who* or *The Generation Game*.

> Asking a fellow teenager in 1977, 'Did you see *The Generation Game*, last night?' was really a rhetorical question. Of course he saw it; what else would he have been doing at Saturday teatime in the middle of winter? Much of what I watch now is on BBC iPlayer or catch-up TV, a DVD or on YouTube. Asking a colleague at work, 'Did you watch a 2001 episode of *Black Books* last night?' would be pretty pointless. Why on earth would he have been watching the same thing as me? (Gillian V. Pettitt)

Because they shared a monopoly, BBC and ITV worked to make sure that didn't waste their time competing with each other needlessly. If the BBC were broadcasting a terrifically popular programme, then ITV would not bother to put anything worth watching on at that time. Both channels worked to this same ethos, with the result that when *Dr Who*, *On the Buses*, *Steptoe & Son* or *The Sweeney* was on, hardly any teenager would be watching the 'other side'. The result has been to give every teenager from that decade a common cultural heritage, at least as far as television is concerned.

I seriously doubt that anybody who was a teenager during the seventies could tell you what was on the other side when *The Generation Game* was on. Any more than you would find somebody who turned over from *Jim'll Fix It* to watch what was on ITV. If you were a young person indoors at certain times of the day, you would be sure to be watching, or even if you weren't watching, then at least hearing in the next room, certain television programmes. They were the one thing that everybody you knew had in common. If you got into a tricky situation at work and said, 'Oooh, Betty!' then everybody would laugh. They knew that you were using a catchphrase from *Some Mothers Do 'Ave 'Em*. So universal was the watching of certain shows during that time, especially by teenagers, that expressions by them were being used all the time, by all your mates. (Martin O'Connell)

9

School

School in the 1970s was a vastly different experience for teenagers than it is now. One change was that as the decade began, the move to comprehensive schools had not yet got fully under way. The majority of teenagers in 1970 were still attending either grammar schools or secondary moderns. The school leaving age in 1970 was still fifteen, which meant that many teenagers of this age started work, rather than continuing at school until they were sixteen or eighteen.

I was at a secondary modern in 1970 and left at fifteen, like most of my mates. We all went off and got jobs. This is something which you can't really imagine today, fifteen year olds working in factories and so on. It sounds like something out of Dickens. Still, that was how it was then. The kids at the grammar schools often stayed on until eighteen, but at secondary moderns most left at fifteen. That's how it was with my brother and me too. (Anon)

Schools were so different in those days. I was at a very old grammar school and the discipline was ferocious, right through the sixth form as well. The cane was used pretty freely and people in my class were still getting beaten when they were fifteen or sixteen. This is something which you just couldn't do today. I don't think you would be able to order a sixteen-year-old boy to bend over now and wait patiently while you whipped him half a dozen times with a piece of bamboo. (Mick Parker)

There were two contrasting experiences of teenage life at school in the early 1970s. On the one hand, if you went to a secondary modern you were likely to be leaving at fifteen and treated as an adult member of the workforce, able to take up any sort of job. On the other hand, if you were at a grammar school it was quite possible that you would remain a schoolchild in uniform right up to the age of eighteen.

Our uniform did not change at all from when I was eight until I left at eighteen; gingham frocks in the summer with white ankle socks, and a skirt in the winter with white knee socks. I am sure that the idea was to keep us under control and doing as we were told. Most sixth forms today have abandoned uniform, because the kids just would not put up with it now. At a very strict boys' school which was near us, even the sixth formers were caned from time to time. We did not really grow up until we left school and for many of us, that was not until we were eighteen. (Polly Reynolds)

Just as teenagers were generally expected to obey their parents in a way that young people today would find surprising, so too were they to do as their teachers told them. The teachers were acting *in loco parentis* and felt that they were entitled to the same level of obedience as a child would display towards his or her parents.

Our school was strict and the teachers could be very unpleasant, but they were only acting as many parents did. Seventeen year olds today think of themselves as adults with all sorts of rights and privileges, but it was a different kettle of fish in the seventies. You tended to do as your father told you and then at school, you did as your teacher told you. They used to back each other up as well, in a kind of conspiracy of adult authority. I know some teachers and they tell me that the parents of teenagers will today come up to the school to complain if they think their child has been unfairly treated. That would have been unthinkable in 1970. Parents and teachers worked together and always backed each other up. (Katherine Cassidy)

Although almost all schools became comprehensive in the 1980s and the selective system all but disappeared, in 1970 this two-tier educational apartheid was still going strong.

I left school in 1970, when I was fifteen, and went to work in a factory. From that moment on, I was an adult. I started smoking, hanging around with the older women and being treated as one of the crowd straight away. My cousin, though, was the same age as me, had passed her 11-plus and was at grammar school. A couple of years after I had left school and had a boyfriend, she was still in school uniform with her plaits tied up with ribbons. It was odd, this division which took place according to whether you went to a grammar or secondary modern. (Anon)

School too was one of those institutions which underwent a dramatic change during the 1970s. By 1980, this division between pupils at secondary moderns and pupils at grammar schools had been swept away. In almost every

part of the country, teenagers were all lumped together
at the same school, usually the local comprehensive. In
1972, the school leaving age was raised to sixteen, and
more teenagers were entering further education by the
end of the decade.

The increasing informality of everyday society was per-
meating secondary schools during the 1970s and enormous
changes were taking place in the experience of teenagers at
school. In 1970, it was still the rule at many schools for
boys in particular to be addressed by their surnames. This
was once common enough in ordinary life in Britain. In
the years following the end of the Second World War, this
custom died out.

> I was at a grammar school from 1965 until 1972. Right up
> until I left the sixth from, most masters would still call us
> by our surnames. It was always Smith or Robinson, very
> seldom Peter or John. We took this for granted, but really
> it was a bit strange because all this had died out years ago
> everywhere else. It wasn't just at grammar schools either,
> I had friends at a secondary modern and it was the same
> there. I never could make up my mind whether this was a
> matter of power, the masters always being called 'Sir' and
> us serfs being called Jones or whatever, or if it was a throw-
> back to the Victorian habit of males addressing each other
> by surnames all the time. (Mick Parker)

> Everything changed in schools during the seventies. I left
> in 1971 and at that time half the masters still wore black
> gowns. It gave the place a very unworldly and scholastic air,
> which was perhaps the whole intention. My brother went
> to the same school in 1979 and the following year I went
> along to his open day with my parents. I cannot tell you

the difference that I saw. None of the masters were wearing gowns and they all called the pupils by their Christian
names. I checked with my brother that this was not just for
the benefit of visiting parents, but he said that it was the
usual thing by then. Also, the cane was hardly being used
at all. When I started at that same school in the sixties, you
could be caned for not doing your homework. By 1981,
caning was reserved only for the most serious offences like
violence or bullying. The boys looked a lot more cheerful
and the whole atmosphere of the place was more open and
good natured. (K.A. Silverstone)

Being a teenager at school in the late 1970s was a completely different thing from what it had been ten years
earlier. Everywhere in the country, there was a trend
towards greater informality and a lessening of the codes
which had held sway since the end of the First World
War. In 1970, a boy could be sent home from school if his
hair was over his collar. By 1979, he was only likely to be
sent home if he turned up sporting a pink mohican. Strict
conformity to certain standards of appearance had largely
melted away.

I left school in 1973. It was a very good girls' grammar
school and the rules on uniform were almost comically
detailed. Our skirts had to be no more than a certain
number of inches above our knees and the deputy head
actually used to check with a tape measure to ensure that
we were not flouting this rule. Ties were worn and the end
had to hang at precisely the right length. Modern teenagers will probably not believe this, but the regulations even
extended to our underwear, with navy blue knickers being
the only acceptable item in that department! Obviously

no jewellery and even the faintest trace of make-up would
be enough for you to be sent either to the washroom to
remove it or to the head to be reproved, depending upon
which teacher detected it. (Theresa O. Littlestone)

By the end of the decade, teenagers at school were being
treated more as young adults than as children. Just as many
parents were beginning to regard their teenage children as
partners and friends, so too did teachers gradually alter
their perception. Teenagers at school, especially those in
the sixth form, were to be consulted and given the respect
due to adults, instead of the paternalistic ordering around
that had been the practice for many decades. Pupils were
fellow human beings now and not awkward young devils
who must be harried and punished into submission so that
they would do as the teacher told them.

I started secondary school in 1973 and didn't leave until
1980. During those years, there were so many changes
that I can hardly list them all. Ours was a comprehensive,
which had formerly been a secondary modern, and it was
mixed. One of the main things which I noticed happening
was that when I began at the school, surnames were generally used for the boys. By the time I left, seven years later,
no teacher would call a pupil by his surname. There was
no official announcement about this; it was just something
which happened. I suppose that the head might have told
the teachers privately or something, but it definitely happened some time round the mid-seventies. I suppose that
this really just mirrored what was going on in the outside
world generally. My father told me that he was called by
his surname at work in the sixties and early seventies and
that this too had changed by 1980. (Sarah P. Moran)

One of the big changes taking place in education at this time, one which affected all teenagers, was the abolition of selective education. From the end of the Second World War up until the late sixties, most children had attended secondary modern schools. Pupils there took different and less academically demanding examinations called the Certificate of Secondary Education (CSE). At grammar schools, the General Certificate of Education (GCE) was taken. During the 1970s, this entire system was dismantled and all pupils at secondary schools were required to sit the same exams. Employers began to ask about qualifications more. At the same time, the old industries were being replaced by services. It would no longer be possible for teenagers to leave school at sixteen and just walk into a job. New skills were needed and an ability to read, write and perform arithmetical calculations was increasingly expected by employers as a basic requirement.

> For years, the boys in our family had just left school a soon as they could at fifteen and found manual work. I thought that it would be the same for me, but by 1978, when I was sixteen, it was all changing. There was unemployment for the first time that anybody could remember. Before then, if you wanted a job it was there for you. Now, I knew young people who were on National Assistance, as they called the dole then. This was a bit of a shock and I was suddenly worried about what would happen when I left school. The answer was to learn a trade and so I went to the technical college for two years to learn motor mechanics. It was a good job that I did, because a lot of the people in my class who left school at sixteen were finding it a real struggle to get a job. After college though, I had skills which people wanted. (Anon)

By the time the 1980s arrived, it was clear that teenagers were no longer assured of a job and for the first time since the 1930s youth unemployment became a problem in this country. Inevitably, this led to more teenagers staying on at school after the age of sixteen in order to acquire qualifications which would give them an advantage in the competition for what jobs were available. This process has continued to this day, until nearly half of all young people attend university. It would have been hard for a teenager in 1970 to envisage such a state of affairs, with jobs so plentiful and employers clamouring for unqualified teenagers to come and work in their factories, shipyards and docks.

10

Work

In the 1970s, as today, starting work was a major mile-
stone in the lives of many teenagers. However, the majority
of people today start work three to five years later than
was the case in 1970.

> When I tell children that I started work in a factory at the
> age of fifteen, they look at me as though I am a survivor
> from the time of Dickens. It was only in 1971 that I left
> school and started work, not really that long ago. I was one
> of the last to start work at fifteen, because the following
> year, the school leaving age was raised to sixteen. At the
> time though, it was the most natural thing in the world for
> boys and girls to leave secondary moderns at fifteen and
> start work instead of going to college or something. (Anon)

As we saw in the previous chapter, the school leaving age
was fifteen up until 1972, with many teenagers staying
on longer than that, usually until they were sixteen. The
number of those who delayed starting work for another
few years has altered radically since the 1970s. It is more or

less taken for granted that, although sixteen is the official age for leaving school, most young people will continue in full-time education beyond this. Going on to college or sixth form is no longer the preserve of a small number of pupils, but has instead become the general rule, rather than the exception.

> Not only did nobody I knew at school go on to university, I don't remember any of my fellow pupils who left in 1971 even going to college. We left school and started work at once. I don't think that my parents would have been too pleased if I had told them that I was going to spend another three or four years studying. It was more or less expected that as soon as you left school, you would be getting a job and contributing to the upkeep of the home. (Anon)

> It was a matter of prestige to my parents that I would be staying on at the sixth form and then going to university. It showed that they did not need me to leave school and get a job and that they were able to support me financially for a few years more. I picked up on this and felt proud of myself. Those of us who went to a sixth form were the special ones. For instance, there was a secondary modern school just down the road from us and this did not have a sixth form. Almost all the pupils there went to work as soon as they were fifteen or sixteen. These days, you would raise your eyes at this. Almost half of all teenagers go on to university; it is a very common event. (Polly Reynolds)

In 1970, fewer than 10 per cent of young people went on to university. Almost all the others started work as soon as they were able to do so. Now, of course, nobody begins work at fifteen, and a there is a small minority who do at sixteen. So, what brought about this change? One of the main changes was that at the beginning of the 1970s this country had full employment and companies were crying out for workers. Factories had notices at their gates advertising vacancies and it was perfectly possible for a teenager to walk out of the house in the morning and have a new job by lunchtime.

> I left school at fifteen, in 1970. There was no question about searching for a job; they were all over the place, wherever you looked. The factory at the end of our street was always looking for people and many shops had signs in their window saying things like, 'Smart young boy wanted'. Most of the time, you didn't even need to fill in an application form; if you had two arms and legs and could stand upright that was it, you were in. The only people in those days to talk about unemployment were parents and grandparents who could remember the Depression. It seemed incredible to us that there should once have been such a state of affairs. True, things had changed a bit by 1979, when Thatcher became Prime Minister. By that time, unemployment was becoming a worry and some teenagers were staying on at college rather than going on the dole. (Anon)

> I don't think that any teenager was out of work in the early seventies, not unless he was idle and did not want a job. This was when there was still a manufacturing industry in this country and factories and dockyards were crying out for unskilled labour. Nobody even asked about qualifications in those days, it didn't matter if you had GCEs or CSEs. The main thing was if you could sit at a conveyor belt or lift heavy weights. (Pat Howard)

At that time, the number of new workers available to industry each year was strictly limited to the number of young people leaving school. This meant that there was no real incentive for the government to expand higher education or encourage schoolchildren to delay the start of their working life. The economic health of the nation depended upon this stream of teenagers leaving school and joining the workforce at once.

> Going to university forty years ago was a rare event in parts of the country like that where I grew up. This was in the North East, round Newcastle. If you lived in some parts of London, going to college and sixth form after the age of sixteen was pretty common, but in my street I was the only one who didn't get a job as soon as I was sixteen. I did well at my GCEs and my parents were determined that I would have the opportunities which they had not had themselves. (Geoffrey C. Feldman)

The move towards getting teenagers to stay on at college or sixth form when they reached sixteen, instead of going straight to work, began in the late 1970s. There were two motives. The first was that as the traditional industries disappeared, jobs which required only a basic, minimum education became scarcer. The new comprehensive schools expected all pupils to take GCEs and so employers began to ask for evidence of educational attainment when taking on school leavers. The new jobs which were being created in services and the commercial world needed a little more than the ability to just lift and carry.

> I grew up near the docks in London. My father and older brother were both dockers and it was natural when I was at school in the sixties that I thought that I would be

following them into the docks. But in the early seventies
came containerisation and the docks moved out to Tilbury
in Essex. At the same time, factories was closing down and
it was becoming harder and harder to find labouring jobs
which required nothing more than physical strength. The
world of work was changing, although we didn't realise it
at the time. When I reached sixteen in 1972, my parents
advised me to go to college and learn a trade. The unskilled
work just wasn't there any more. (David Ford)

Economic conditions also meant that unemployment
began to increase from around 1974 onwards. This
became a hot political topic and there was pressure on
successive governments to try and reduce the level of
unemployment. Since creating jobs out of thin air was not
always possible, one way to reduce the figures was to get
more school leavers to stay in further education and attend
technical colleges and sixth forms.

The situation for teenagers getting a job changed dramatically between 1970, when my brother left school, and 1978,
when I left. In 1970, there was still full employment and
school leavers were encouraged to get out into the world
and get a job at once. When I turned sixteen at the beginning of 1978, unemployment was rising sharply and many
of the jobs had just disappeared. I was in competition with
older men for the available unskilled work. Some school
leavers were advised to go on to college to get a qualifica-
tion or two. We were told that this would give us an edge in
the job market. (Anon)

It was widely assumed that girls and boys would be doing
different jobs when they left school. Magazines like *Jackie*

reinforced this feeling, with advertisements for touch typing courses and opportunities to train to be nurses.

An issue of *Jackie* in April 1975 provided an insight into the world of work as most teenage girls would more realistically experience it. It was an advertisement in the form of a strip cartoon. The first frame shows half a dozen girls working in the typing pool, each seated at a desk with a typewriter. One of the girls is saying to her friend, 'I'd love to get a new job'. They look at the noticeboard and see that there is a vacancy for a receptionist, but as the girl explains, 'I haven't got the confidence to apply. My skin is so dull and lifeless.' Fortunately, the girl's friend tells her about Anne French deep cleansing milk, which removes 'Every trace of grime and stale make-up, leaving your skin healthy and clean.' With her newly clean face and boosted confidence, the girl gets the job as the receptionist. Her reward is shown in the final frame; here she is, sitting in reception looking clean and attractive. Two smart young executives are standing near her desk, obviously within earshot, and one is saying to the other, 'Look at that smashing new bird in reception.' In response to this, she is shown as thinking, 'I love this new job. You meet so many interesting people'.

11

Belongings

Not surprisingly, the technological advances of the 1970s which were thought of as new and invigorating have changed beyond all recognition into the technology we use today. However, gadgets and devices from the 1970s were considered more of a precious commodity to many teenagers at that time.

> Nothing infuriates me more than seeing my children being careless with possessions which, when I was a teenager, I would have treasured. Everything they own is somehow seen as being disposable and if lost can be replaced almost at once. Cameras, watches, radios, telephones; you name it and my teenage children have either trodden on it in their bedroom, left it round a friend's house or forgotten to bring it home from school at the end of term. They just do not value all the luxuries that they have now. (Maria T. Valentine)

Having a wristwatch was seen as a rite of passage in the early 1970s, with children seldom being trusted with a watch before their teenage years. They were to be found only in jewellers' shops, and were invariably clockwork watches that one had to remember to wind each night before going to bed. One took great care of a watch, because it was valuable and could not easily be replaced; a watch that was lost or stolen might mean that you would just have to go without until you could afford a new one.

> I remember my first watch. I got it as a Christmas present in 1971 when I was thirteen. It was nothing special, just gold plated, but it still cost five guineas. I suppose that would be about £60 or £70 in today's value. Our school had a rule that pupils were not allowed to wear watches for school, in case anything happened to them. I wore it everywhere else though and felt very grown-up. I was begging for somebody to ask me what the time was for the first few weeks after I got it. (Terry Barlow)

> I was given one of the new digital watches for my fourteenth birthday in 1977 and I was the envy of my friends. My parents were uneasy about my wearing it to school, but I was so pleased with it and could not wait to show it off. Nobody else in my class had such a thing; they all had wind-up watches. I treasured that watch. (Sarah P. Moran)

Contrast this with the situation today, where watches are available as fashion accessories in many shops. It is the same story with other gadgets; cameras, for example. At one time, the average family perhaps owned just one, which would be used by the parents on holidays and special occasions. If a teenager wanted to own a camera of their own, then they would have to save up for it or perhaps ask for it as a birthday or Christmas present. Films were expensive as well, as was the cost of developing the photographs. During the late 1960s and early 1970s, cheaper cameras came onto the market. These were, essentially, updated versions of the old box brownie cameras that their parents had used when they were young – fixed focus and aperture box cameras, which could only be used in bright sunlight. The Kodak Instamatic was a very popular model.

> I remember getting an Instamatic outfit for my birthday. I was dead keen on taking up photography as a hobby and begged my parents to buy me a camera. For my fifteenth birthday I got this big box containing an Instamatic, a case and wrist strap for it, and a film. It was the deluxe model, with a flash. I can still remember the excitement of having a camera of my own. (Katherine Cassidy)

> I really cannot imagine anybody throwing a perfectly good camera away when I was a teenager. It would have been absolutely mad. Even if you didn't want it yourself, you would give or sell it to somebody. These days though, my children started off with cameras which took film and they then graduated to digital cameras. Now, they only use their mobiles. The only thing one can do is to chuck out the old ones. Who would want a digital camera from 2001, one with a proper viewfinder that you peer through and really chunky buttons? An eleven-year-old camera in 1973 would be as good as the latest model. The technology of the things did not change overnight as it seems to these days. (Nina Webb)

Along with cameras and watches, record players were also valued possessions of the 1970s teenager.

> I remember buying my first stereo when I was nineteen. It cost about £100 and at that time I was only earning about £10 or £12 a week. I suppose this would have been in the

mid-seventies. There was no question of buying the thing
outright, I had to get it on the 'never-never', what used to
be called hire purchase. I can tell you, I took fanatically
good care of that deck and speakers. I kept it dusted and
cleaned with special stuff. I wouldn't let my mother touch it
when she was cleaning my bedroom. It took me six months
to pay for it, but it was money well spent; definitely my
favourite possession for a year or two. (David Ford)

Teenagers' belongings at the time were very much in the
nature of being 'one-offs'. This applied to everything from
cameras to the photographs taken with them, stereos to
records, watches to bicycles. If you lost a favourite photograph of your girlfriend, then it was gone for good.
Photographs were expensive to have developed and often
the negatives were later mislaid. A handwritten letter from
a lover was a precious thing, of which good care might be
taken for years. It was, after all, irreplaceable.

As a result, teenagers in the 1970s had caches of tangi-
ble mementos which they kept hold of and in some cases
still have. A letter written from a seaside resort in 1972, a
photograph from a holiday in 1976, a first watch, an old
LP with no means of playing it; a lot of people who were
teenagers in the 1970s have collections of this sort.

I had a holiday romance in 1978, when I was fifteen. It was in
Spain and he was a waiter at our hotel. Apart from my memories, there is one faded and blurry snapshot taken by my father,
in which the boy can just be glimpsed in the background.
Everything in those days was so ephemeral and fleeting. If I
could see a detailed account of my holiday romance thirty-five
years ago, together with high definition images and colour
film, it would destroy the magic. (Maria T. Valentine)

Today, teenagers can communicate via texts, emails, Facebook, and Twitter; they can send photographs from their mobile phones to all of their friends. This is a completely different way of communication than that of the 1970s. The drunken, late night phone call made to a girlfriend in 1974 left no record, save in the memory. Nowadays, the drunken, late night text, email or comment left on somebody's Facebook wall can haunt everyone involved for quite some time.

> If you rang somebody and told them that you loved them or hated them or anything else, it didn't really matter a few days later. Chances were, only you and the person concerned would know the truth about it. Most of my conversations were with small groups of friends and although some people might later gossip, it was easy to deny what you might have said. After all, there was no permanent record. (Mary A. Barker)

Unlike today's throw-away fashion, clothes were also deemed as precious belongings for teenagers in the 1970s. Today, teenagers have a vast and wide array of clothes to choose from, whereas things were somewhat different forty years ago.

> I only had one decent jacket when I was eighteen. I had one pair of shoes for work and another for going out in the evenings. In general, my friends and I had only one or two of everything; from jeans to pairs of shoes. Clothes and shoes were mended and we took care of them. As far as make-up was concerned, I had a lipstick, two eyeshadows, and one mascara. Pinching make-up from Boots was the commonest form of dishonesty in which we would be involved in the seventies. Make-up was so expensive and we so desperately

wanted to have it that nicking it from a chemist seemed to
be the best way of laying our hands on it. (Polly Reynolds)

Growing up, I would receive gifts of clothing for birthdays
and Christmas. Not designer clothing or expensive trainers
or anything, but jumpers and coats. There was more money
about in the late seventies, but for many people, money was
pretty tight at that time and kids had a lot fewer possessions than they do now. (Martin O'Connell)

So, what would a typical 1970's teenager's bedroom con-
tain? Well, there would of course be the bed itself; almost
invariably covered with a candlewick bedspread! Beyond
that, a chest of drawers or dressing table and perhaps a
wardrobe; there would usually be little else. There might
have been a record player, often one which had been
handed down by parents. In the later 1970s, this might
perhaps have been supplemented by a portable cassette
player with a radio, and there might have been a camera,
a few items of make-up, if a girl, and of course posters on
the wall of pop stars or footballers and that would pretty
much be it.

My youngest son went off to university last year and I
remember looking sadly round his room after he had
packed up and left for Leeds. Now remember that this was
after he had left and taken his belongings with him. He left
behind two digital cameras, a mobile phone, two calculators, an MP3 player with a radio, a radio cassette player, a
colour television, a video player and a computer. Any one
of these objects would have been a prized possession to a
teenager in the 1970s, something to be longed for and perhaps received as a Christmas present. (Katherine Cassidy)

A shift has taken place in how teenagers today regard the things that they own, compared with the generation before them. The average lifespan of a mobile telephone or digital camera owned by a teenager is only a year or two. A camera owned by a thirteen year old in 1971 would still be being used when the person was nineteen in 1977. They would be fiercely protective of their possessions, and it would be a rare teenager indeed who would leave a camera on the floor of his or her bedroom for somebody to accidentally to step on.

> I remember my first proper 35mm camera, which I had for my fifteenth birthday in 1974. Before that I had an Instmatic, but this was one with variable focus, adjustable aperture and all the rest of it. I took such care of that camera, polishing the lens, keeping it in its leather case at all times and the whole thing stored in the cardboard box in which it came, along with the instruction booklet. I had a much better camera than anybody else I knew and I can truthfully say that it was a prized possession. (Theresa O. Littlestone)

In the 1970s, when something got broken or stopped working, then it would be mended and continue to be used. Today, technology changes so fast that, in some cases, it is easier to just buy a new item instead of getting it fixed.

> My father used to type letters on an old, manual typewriter. He had had it since the war and it was still going strong in the early 1980s. The same thing with his camera, which was a very sturdy thing which he had had since the end of the Second World War. Of course, the technology of typewriters and cameras had not changed and so it seemed natural to him to carry on using the things until they broke.

> I think that those of us who grew up at that time, during the
> sixties and seventies, picked up something of that feeling.
> I still hate throwing away anything which is still working,
> it seems so extravagant. There was still a bit of a feeling of
> 'make do and mend' as the seventies started. (Mick Parker)

Before the 1970s, watches and cameras, gramophones
and radios, telephones, typewriters and almost everything
else had been developing slowly along the same lines since
the end of Queen Victoria's reign. With the introduction
of transistor radios in America in the late 1950s, technology began to change from mechanical to electronic. This
meant that new gadgets would be superseded within a
year or two by new models. The differences between
the new models and the old ones were more than merely
cosmetic. The new versions of radios and telephones were
actually better than the old and made the existing versions
outdated. The first push button telephone to appear in
this country, the Trimphone, differed not just in appearance but in its basic mechanism.

12

Relaxing

Financial constraints dictated the ways in which 1970s teenagers spent their spare time. Much of what teenagers and young people did in those days had to be free or at the very least extremely cheap.

> In the seventies, a lot of socialising took place in each other's bedrooms. A few friends would come round and we would sit up there listening to records or the radio. That was most of my socialising as a teenager in, say, 1978. If I wanted a coffee, then of course I could go downstairs and make one, but the idea of popping out to have a coffee just for the sake of it would have been ludicrous. Apart from the odd trip to the pictures at the weekend, most of my spare time when I was fourteen or fifteen didn't cost a penny. (Katherine Cassidy)

Younger teenagers would have to get by on practically nothing for their day-to-day life. This explains, in part, why things such as church youth clubs were still going strong in the 1970s. They were a place to hang out with friends and the cost was only nominal.

I used to go to the youth club at our local church until I was seventeen. It was something to do on one evening a week and better than staying indoors with my parents. A lot of us used to belong to the youth club and it was a condition of membership that you had to attend church at least once a month. Although the average age was probably around fourteen or fifteen, there was a fair sprinkling of older kids of sixteen or seventeen. Going to the pub could be expensive and for those of us who were still at school, the money just wasn't there for us to go out all the time. The church youth club was at least somewhere to go, something to do. (Pat Howard)

Today, the old-style church youth club has all but disappeared. With so many exciting things to do at home, many teenagers feel there is no reason to venture out of the house unless there is something particularly interesting to attract them. The family home has become a pretty attractive place for many modern teenagers in a way that would have been impossible to understand for the teenagers of forty years ago; after all, what was there for a sixteen year old to do in their bedroom in 1970? They might play a record, although they would be unlikely to have more than a dozen at the most. The television was downstairs and under the control of the parents. There would be no personal telephone, no Internet, no computer games, no DVDs; only a few posters on the walls to look at and perhaps a book to read. No wonder that teenagers in the '70s didn't really want to spend all that much time alone in their rooms!

A lot more teenagers belonged to uniformed organisations like the Scouts, Boys' Brigade and Girl Guides when I was a teenager. They were cheap and it was something to do in the evenings. My own children did not want to do anything as old-fashioned as being in the Guides, mainly because there were so many more things that they could do when they were teenagers. (Mary A. Barker)

Something that people forget is that there really wasn't much to do in the average house if you were a teenager in the seventies. Obviously, there were no computers, DVD players or games consoles; in the average house there would be one black and white television and maybe a stereo and a radio. That was about it. This is why teenagers had hobbies; it gave them something to do in the evenings and at weekends. I did bell ringing until I was eighteen and there were a few other boys there who went along one evening a week to practice. It wasn't much of an entertainment, but it was better than staying indoors on Tuesday evenings. It was dull at home and we didn't have loads of money to be always going to the cinema and so on. (David Ford)

Much of the socialising and leisure activities of teenagers during the 1970s cost, quite literally, nothing at all to do. The computers and mobile phones of today did not exist then and so, invariably, conversations were mainly held face-to-face.

My friends and I were always talking and these long conversations used to take place all over the place. In each others' bedrooms, while sitting in the park, having a coffee in Lyons; face-to-face conversations were our main pastime. I went from sixth form to university in the early seventies and so as a teenager I had very little money to spend. It would have been no use asking my mother every five minutes for money to go out, she simply didn't have it.

> Talking to people who are only a few feet from you is an
> entirely different thing from sending emails or texting.
> (Christopher Walker)

A consequence of this was that trips to the pictures and
days out had a certain vividness to them. In the early
1970s, most teenagers saw films only in black and white.
Perhaps once or twice a year they would have the experience of seeing a film in full colour. Such events were special
and eagerly anticipated.

> When I was teenager we only had a black and white TV
> at home and I didn't get to go to the cinema all that often.
> Seeing a film in Technicolor was a real pleasure when I was
> a teenager. These days, kids that age take regular visits to
> the cinema and films on demand for granted. (Nina Webb)

In those days, teenagers were frequently thrown back on
their own resources and found that they had to find ways
to entertain themselves. Sitting in bedrooms and talking to
one or two friends was one of those free ways of passing
the time which almost everybody who was a teenager in
the 1970s will recall.

> There was an intensity to even our casual conversations
> which I don't see among young people today, including my
> own children. In the seventies, we were passionately con-
> nected with the people to whom we were close. This was a
> consequence of both the technology, or lack of it, at the time,
> and also various other things. When you were with some-
> body, you were absolutely with them; completely connected.
> (Katherine Cassidy)

Younger teenagers were allowed a considerable amount of freedom by their parents in the 1970s. Young teenagers would often be seen be wandering around with each other, unaccompanied. Groups of thirteen year olds on choppers would ride round car parks or waste grounds, just enjoying each other's company.

> I know that it is something of a cliché for middle-aged men and women to talk of leaving the house in the morning and not returning until teatime, when they were hungry, but this was really the case when I was fourteen or so. We had no money and just went off with our bikes for the day. We didn't get into much trouble; it was just such fun to be in our own world, without adults to poke their noses in. My parents weren't on the phone and they could not have contacted me even if they'd wanted to. The people that I hung around with then would probably be called a 'gang' these days. We didn't do any harm and the friendships we formed lasted. (Paul Clarke)

Relaxation for this generation of teenagers typically relied upon their own imagination and freedom. In the 1970s, boredom was a powerful driving force.

> What I most remember from my teenage years, 1970-7, is people, mainly my friends. I don't have such clear memories of things, like record players or televisions say. These were not the main things in my life; it was people who mattered and people that I remember most vividly. (Terry Barlow)

13

The Generation Gap

During the 1960s, the so-called generation gap became a recognised phenomenon in Western society. The idea was that as the 'baby boomer' generation became teenagers, they were rebelling against their parents' values and also traditional society in general. They listened to different music, dressed in strange and alarming ways, experimented with drugs and were sexually promiscuous. This behaviour was in sharp contrast to that of their parents and there was, accordingly, a gulf between middle-aged parents and their teenage offspring.

I went to college to study art in 1970, when I was eighteen. There could hardly have been a greater difference between my way of life and that of my parents. My father used to wear a collar and tie, even on picnics, and he had his hair cut at least once a month! Most of my boyfriends never used to have their hair cut and had not worn a tie since leaving school. My parents could not bear the sound of the music I listened to; they preferred classical stuff. They often talked of a 'proper job'; meaning one where one would be

wearing a suit and working from nine to five. They also
disapproved strongly of sex before marriage. I was on the
pill at that time and had had a number of boyfriends. The
generation gap was certainly a good way to describe our
family set-up. (Katherine Cassidy)

This was not an uncommon situation at the start of the
decade. Even in homes where the children were not rebel-
lious students, parents had the impression that teenagers
were somehow rising up in opposition to them and that
the different generations were actually in conflict. This
concept provided the name for one of the most popular
television programmes of the 1970s; Bruce Forsyth's *The
Generation Game*, which first appeared in 1971.

I got the impression that my parents and their friends felt
that their whole way of life and all their values were being
challenged and in danger of being destroyed by the young
people who were then growing to adulthood. They didn't
often state this explicitly, you just had the feeling that they
thought that their way of life was under siege. I suppose
this might account for the way that they reacted in the early
seventies to things like the length of my hair and the clothes
which I wore. The overall atmosphere was one of confrontation between teenagers and their parents. I certainly don't
feel like this with my own teenage children. (Paul Clarke)

When the 1970s began, an awful lot of parents were deeply
suspicious and mistrustful of teenagers and their 'strange'
new ways. Middle aged and older people reacted by fiercely
denouncing much of what they thought young people were
advocating; whether it be fashions in hair length, styles
of clothing, sexual morality or tastes in music. What is

interesting to note is that this apparent battle between the
generations was over by the end of the 1970s and resulted
in a complete rout for the older generation!

> I was sixteen in 1970, the year that I left school. At that
> time, I was constantly fighting with my parents about
> wearing jeans all the time and not having my hair cut as
> short as my father. There were also rows about what they
> saw as my immorality; they discovered that I was sleeping
> with my girlfriend and couldn't understand why I had no
> plans to marry her. Things could hardly have been more
> different by 1980. By that time, my father was himself
> wearing jeans at the weekend and listening cheerfully
> to 'pop' music, if only ABBA. His hair was now over
> his collar and my sister was living, unmarried, with her
> boyfriend. There had been a sea change in the attitudes of
> older people over those ten years. (Mick Parker)

There is no doubt that teenagers were the driving force
behind many of the changes which took place in British
society during the 1970s. The music they favoured was
increasingly heard, not just on Radio 1 but also as the
soundtrack to documentaries and films. The old 'short
back and sides' hairstyle had practically disappeared by
the end of the 1970s, lingering on only in a few diehards.
Facial hair sprouted on many men. Bruce Forsyth and
The Generation Game provides a perfect example of the
changes taking place in styles and fashions at that time;
changes which have had a long-lasting effect to this very
day. The bushy sideboards which Bruce Forsyth sported in
the 1970s were something of a *leit motif* of that era. Until
the 1960s, respectable men were usually clean-shaven
with the short back and sides. With pop singers and their

teenage followers allowing facial hair to flourish in the late 1960s, many older men felt that the conventions were beginning to loosen a little and that it was now permissible to experiment a little bit. Typically, this manifested itself as sideboards and moustaches; both a very 1970s thing for men, particularly those approaching middle age.

> Attitudes of older people altered drastically over the seventies. I saw it in my own parents. At the end of the sixties they were dead set against anything like long hair, pop music, men dressing in what they regarded as a slovenly fashion, girls not wearing skirts; there was a list as long as your arm. By the eighties, this had all changed. Both my mother and father were dressing more casually, they were not moaning about pop music all the time, nor were they complaining about long-haired men. It seemed to me that they had accepted a lot of teenage culture and more or less adopted it themselves. (Esther M. Hannigan)

As the 1970s progressed, the whole idea of a generation gap faded away, partly because of the increasing tendency of older men and women to act as though they were themselves teenagers.

> I suppose that I noticed by 1980 that my mother was trying to be a little bit younger than her actual age. It was nothing dramatic; she would dress more casually and try to enjoy the music that I enjoyed. The other thing I noticed was that whereas ten years earlier she had been very contemptuous about teenage slang, she was now making a conscious effort to pick it up and use it. Of course, a lot of it was behind the times by then. The overall impression was that she had decided that being young was a good thing and that

looking and talking a bit more like a teenager might be a
desirable thing for her. (Sarah P. Moran)

Much of the way that parents and other adults related to
teenagers during the 1970s was an extension of what had
begun in the 1960s. The 'baby boom', after the end of the
Second World War, had produced a population explosion
which translated into greatly increased numbers of teenagers in Britain during the 1960s and '70s. There had been
previous 'baby booms' however, and it might all have
passed without note, except for the fact that the generation
of teenagers who emerged at this time were not content
with the old ways of life which they inherited. The sight of
all these weird looking young people must certainly have
been alarming to parents who had, in the main, just grown
up and copied the ways that their own parents dressed,
spoke and behaved.

> My parents always managed to give me the idea that I had
> somehow let them down. Not getting a job as soon as I
> left school was a warning sign to them. Then, when I let
> my hair grow a bit longer once I was a student that was
> another black mark. Listening to noisy pop music whose
> lyrics all seemed to be about drugs didn't help matters. The
> overall picture was that they had left school and knuckled
> down, behaving like respectable people and following in
> their parents' footsteps. But that wasn't good enough for
> me; I had to try and revolutionise society. (K.A. Silverstone)

There are a number of reasons why we no longer have a
generation gap between teenagers and their parents, of the
sort which existed in the 1970s. For the first twenty years
or so after the end of the Second World War things carried

on pretty much the same way as they had always done. When the 'baby boom' generation became teenagers, they wanted something a little different from the bleak, post-war world into which they had been born. In turn, this led to some of the changes previously mentioned, namely the distinctive groupings of teenagers and an unwillingness to abide by the rules and conventions which had governed the lives of their parents.

> When I was a teenager during the seventies my parents' attitude could be summed up as, 'It was good enough for my parents; it is good enough for us; why should you be any different?' and 'Our ancestors behaved in such and such a way, we have never questioned this and so why should you now do so?' Against that kind of mindset, there is little that can be done. I do know that this is not how the parents I now know think. The fact that my grandfather did things in a certain way or dressed in a particular style has no bearing at all on how my children should be living their lives. Why should it? Yet in the seventies, parents still tried this line all the time. No wonder that as teenagers we used to get frustrated and angry. (David Ford)

So why do parents today feel differently? Perhaps it is partly because they were the ones who led the rebellion and many of them have a clear memory of what it was like to feel that one's aspirations were being suppressed by a bunch of old fogies! Another reason could be the large scale immigration of the 1950s and '60s, which transformed British society from the grey, homogenous mass of the 1950s into a variety of multi-cultural communities, each with their own customs, languages and ways of dressing. Today, there is no longer such dull conformity against

which teenagers can rebel and so the war between the
generations has more or less ended.

> I remember when I was seventeen; a friend of mine joined
> the Hare Krishna people who used to parade down Oxford
> Street chanting. This was a pretty horrifying event for his
> parents, since the default religion for 'normal' people in
> those days, 1971, was Church of England. Today, convert-
> ing to Islam, copying the fashions of the Rastafarians by
> having dreadlocks, becoming a Buddhist or vegetarian;
> all these things happen every day with teenagers. With so
> many cultures flourishing in the country now, parents are
> far more tolerant when their teenagers choose to follow a
> slightly different path to their own. (Mick Parker)

> I remember when I was fifteen I decided to become vegetar-
> ian. You might have thought that I had announced that I
> intended to enter a convent or have my arm amputated. My
> parents took it as a personal affront that I should no longer
> want to eat dead animals. I was not pressing them to abandon
> meat, but it was just the idea that I should want to eat differ-
> ently from them. It was not as common in the late seventies
> to be a vegetarian as it is now and there was certainly not
> the wide range of products available that there is now, but I
> don't think that it was any slight inconvenience about food
> preparation which annoyed them. It was just the sheer fact
> that I did not want to eat the same things as them, the same
> as their parents and their grandparents had eaten for years.
> (Maria T. Valentine)

By the end of the decade, not only were parents a little
less quick to condemn their teenage children for deviating
from the norm, but they had even taken on board some

of the new ideas which their children were embracing and adopted them for their own use. The sexual revolution, for instance, started in the late 1960s, had triumphed by 1980 to the extent that many middle-aged people had become converts to the cause!

> Something which I did pick up when I was teenager was that my own parents had not rebelled against societal norms to anything like the degree that we did. Studying British history at A Level led me to the same conclusion. For hundreds of years, there had been a ban on pre-marital sex, adultery, homosexuality, babies born outside marriage and a host of other things. The seventies saw all this change in a few years; traditions dating back to the Anglo-Saxons, just scrapped. This was not a temporary change; it has gathered strength since then to the extent that we now have a Conservative Prime Minister [David Cameron] championing gay marriage. The 1970s saw the abandonment of a code of morality a thousand years old and the whole business was triggered off by us, the teenagers. (Polly Reynolds)

It is a matter of common observation that any number of things which had still been going strong in this country for years, had fallen from favour by the end of the 1970s. The stigma attached to having a baby out of wedlock, premarital or extramarital sexual activity, living together before marriage, having a string of sexual partners, divorce, gay sex; all these were regarded by most adults as being immoral during the 1960s. By the time the 1980s had arrived there had been a shift and most people accepted or even practiced a new code of morality.

14

The Alternative Society

Since the end of the Second World War teenagers were known to rebel against the majority of things in which their parents' generation believed. This opposition to tradition was, until around 1970, completely negative. A lot of teenagers did not approve of their parents and older people in general, and felt that society was in a pretty awful state and were determined that they would not allow themselves to end up like their parents. In the 1950s and '60s, this rejection of conventional values manifested itself in a variety of nihilistic youth movements such as the Teddy Boys, beatniks, mods and rockers. This destructive attitude was epitomised in the 1953 film *The Wild One*, where the leader of a gang of bikers is asked, 'What are you rebelling against?' He replies, 'What have you got?'

> I remember my older brother in the late 1960s. He was against everything which our parents' generation stood for and yet it was all negative. He was just against them and all they stood for. There was no sense that he should be expected to come up with any alternative, it was enough for him just to

sneer at what they believed in. When I began college in 1970,
I fell in with people who also were dissatisfied with what their
parents and society as a whole were for, but these people were
looking for another way of life. They were searching for a
viable alternative to straight society. (Mick Parker)

As the 1970s began, some teenagers and young people
became dissatisfied with simply being opposed to everything for the sake of it and tried to set about constructing
a credible alternative to the society in which they had
grown up. This movement became known as the 'alternative society'. There were many strands to the alternative
society, which was part of a wider counter-culture which
had begun in America. It is accordingly very hard to define
what these teenagers did actually stand for. However,
despite the fragmented nature of this movement, most of
those taking part had at least a few points in common.

I hung around with quite a few students when I was fifteen
or sixteen. My first boyfriend was a student. This was in
1971, I think, and the people I mixed with were a few
years older than me, say eighteen or nineteen. They all
had roughly similar views. They didn't approve of the
nuclear family, were dead set against capitalism, in favour
of communal living and thought that everybody should
have sex whenever they wanted and be free to take drugs
if they felt like it. As far as I could see, that was about the
limit of their ideology. (Polly Reynolds)

Many young people at this time honestly thought that
the society into which they had been brought up had
failed in some way. Not only had it produced a generation with hang-ups about sex but it also encouraged greed.

Family life was felt to be especially pernicious and should, at least according to some of these radical young people, be replaced by a communal lifestyle.

> This was a time that saw the setting up of communes, where young people could live freely without the pressures of family life and straight society. I moved into a commune in 1971 after a couple of years of rowing with my parents about everything from the length of my hair to what subjects I wanted to study at college. I was seventeen. At first, it was like one long holiday. The other people living there were a couple of years older than me and they never did much, apart from deal a bit of dope, steal from shops and sign on once a week. The place was a squat and there was always the uncertainty hanging over us that the bailiffs would arrive. I soon discovered that with no washing machine, the only way to clean my clothes was to wash them in a bowl of cold water. There was no heating or hot water in the place. It was great that summer, but by the autumn I had had enough and moved back home. (Mick Parker)

Many of the communes set up in the early 1970s were unbelievably squalid and overcrowded. The unattractive and insanitary state of such places tended to be a kind of test – obviously, only those with hopelessly outdated and bourgeois views would object to having no hot water or being obliged to use a bath which had not been cleaned for several months!

> I really would not like to describe in detail what it was like at the abandoned East End pub that we took over in 1972 to found a commune. We managed to get the water turned

on, but electricity was harder. For the first month, we only had candles and paraffin lamps. Eventually, we managed to persuade the Electricity Board to connect us, whereupon one of the guys, who had worked as an electrician, managed to bypass the meter so that we were not actually paying for the power. We soon found that all sorts of waif and strays were attracted to us and at one point there were over twenty people sleeping in five rooms. Nobody wanted to clean and so we set up a house committee. This ended up with some of the founding members of the commune, like me, being denounced as fascists. Who else but a fascist would try to organise a rota for cleaning the bath? Great days while they lasted. (K.A. Silverstone)

It is significant that quite a few of the ideas which those in favour of the alternative society advocated, like the abolition of marriage, free love and so on, have actually arrived since the 1970s. It is impossible to say how much subsequent changes in society's attitudes were affected by the ideologies circulating among radical teenagers in that decade. At the very least, it is probably fair to say that many of what were, at the time, viewed as extremist or hopelessly utopian ideas have now come to be generally accepted by mainstream society.

15

We're All Teenagers Now

When the 1970s began, there were sharp divisions between children, teenagers and adults. These separate categories were marked by clothing, hairstyle, and taste in music, among many other things. For example, a teenage girl would usually wear her hair long and loose, whereas her mother would almost invariably have hers short and possibly permed. The middle-aged woman with long flowing hair was an oddity in 1970. Children dressed in a completely different way from teenagers as well. There was a definite transition which took place when an adolescent girl began wearing high heels, nylons and make-up. These outward distinctions had existed in this country in one form or another for centuries.

Looking at my family photograph album, it is very clear that at least as far back as my grandparents at the end of the nineteenth century, children and adults dressed and looked differently. In our family now, this is not really the case at all. We all wear more or less the same type of clothes. You see it on the streets, girls of seven wearing things that could pass

for teenage styles. What is even odder is that their mothers
are also often wearing the same sort of thing; clothes that
would look OK on a fifteen year old. (Mary A. Barker)

One of the social changes which took place in the 1970s
was the blurring of separate categories for the appearance of
children, adults and adolescents. In 1969, an eleven-year-old
girl wearing high heels or make-up would have presented
a shocking sight. A middle-aged mother wearing jeans and
with long hair down her back would have caused raised eyebrows in the late sixties, but this too has become the norm.

> I know exactly what my mother looked like when she was
> my daughter's age. I know, because I have old photographs
> of her standing next to me when I was myself nineteen. The
> contrast between those family pictures from the seventies and
> the way that I dress now is unbelievable. My hair is very long,
> my mothers by contrast is short and permed. Her clothes at
> fifty are the sort of thing that you would expect somebody in
> an old people's home to be wearing now; certainly not any-
> body of my age. Her whole air is of middle age, approaching
> old age. This is really not how I see myself at the same age!
> (Esther M. Hannigan)

Of course, styles of clothes change over the years. It would
be surprising if people were not dressing differently today
than they were forty years ago; clothes in the 1970s were
quite different from those in the 1930s, which were in turn
nothing like those of the 1890s. Where things have changed,
though, is that at all times in the past there have been dis-
tinguishing features for the clothing and appearance of
children, adolescents, young adults and middle-aged people,
it is those clear distinctions that have crumbled away.

In our family, there is me, I am forty-seven, and my two
children; one of whom is a ten-year-old girl and the other
a fourteen-year-old boy. In the 1970s, my daughter would,
at ten, have been skipping around in a ladybird dress and
wearing white ankle socks, probably with her hair in plaits.
In fact, she dresses more like a teenager than anything else.
I buy her stuff from New Look and what is really strange is
that I also get myself clothes from there – a woman of forty-
seven and a ten year old both dressing in similar styles.
You can't imagine that happening in 1975, when I was ten.
(Maria T. Valentine)

For most of this country's history, the tastes and behaviour
of young adults, even before the expression 'teenagers' was
coined some time in the 1940s, was regarded with some
disdain by adults and it was assumed that young people
would eventually settle down and behave like adults.

Both my son and daughter are now in their early twenties.
When they were in their teens, I made an effort to get on
well, often by acting a little younger than my age. I would
listen to their music and try to be what my own parents
would have called 'with it'. Many of my friends were the
same and all of us have tried to be less like authoritarian
parents and more like friends to our children. I avoided
showing disapproval and tried to understand how my kids
felt. (Theresa O. Littlestone)

Before 1970, a strict set of taboos had been in place for
centuries, which governed the sexual mores of Britain.
These taboos might, from time to time, have been evaded
or defied, but they remained more or less intact from Tudor
times until the 1960s.

The so-called 'sexual revolution', which was spearheaded by teenagers in the late 1960s and early 1970s, did away with the conventions to which almost every adult had previously adhered. Today, only the most religious or conservative of people would regard pre-marital sex as anything other than a normal and healthy activity between adults. The ideological objections to the nuclear family which were raised by those championing the alternative society have almost become the new orthodoxy, with marriage rejected by some as an outmoded institution.

> Something which I have noticed is that a lot of the things which we fought for as students in the early seventies are now almost universal. We said that the family was the cause of most hang-ups and that it would be better if people just had temporary partners and helped raise each other's children. This happens all the time these days. Women are no longer chained to the house and are not forced to just raise and care for their own children, they have careers too. Forty years ago, when we were putting forward this radical agenda, it was thought that this would create a generation of children who were more socialised and less aggressive, with fewer neuroses. (Christopher Walker)

In some instances, what was once seen as extreme teenage activism in the 1970s has now become mainstream thinking today; for example, the move towards legalising gay marriage. This is a direct result of the ideas expressed by the Gay Liberation Front in the early 1970s.

16

The Teenage Tribes of the 1970s

The various groups of teenagers who were so visible in the 1970s, all had their roots in earlier subcultures. The difference was that they had vastly expanded from being a tiny handful of atypical individuals on the fringe of society until they had many thousands of adherents and included teenagers from all walks of life.

I became a punk in 1978, when I was seventeen. My father was an accountant and a Conservative councillor. When I was younger, he used to speak disparagingly about 'beatniks' and 'yobbos'. He associated them with a particular kind of working-class youth. Now, here was a member of his own middle-class family with spiky pink hair and a safety pin through her ear in place of the neat gold studs which I had previously worn. As for so many respectable parents at that time, what had previously been something he read about in the papers had taken root in his own home! (Mary A. Barker)

My parents were delighted at the idea of my going to university, but horrified at the thought of me becoming a student.

Today, the word 'student' does not have such negative connotations as it did in the early seventies. When my father was
at Cambridge before the war, he just studied law and went
punting. Students in 1971 were a strange breed of young
people who were always picketing embassies, smoking
drugs and trying to bring down the government. They had
long hair and revolutionary ideas. So, while my parents were
pleased enough at my being offered a place at university, they
did not want me to turn into a student. (Christopher Walker)

Most of these 'tribes' had their origins in earlier teenage
styles. The skinheads were the descendents of the mods,
who in their turn had morphed from the Teddy Boys of
the 1950s. The hippies had their roots in the beatniks of
the 1950s and the bikers were derived from the rockers,
greasers and Hell's Angels of earlier years.

When I was a kid, this was in the early sixties and so I was
eight or nine, I remember going to the pictures with my
parents and seeing a black and white British film which featured some art students. They were referred to as 'beatniks'
and they looked as though they were having a great time.
The men had beards and the girls wore unconventional
clothes. I thought then that I would like to be like that when
I grew up. A few years later when the hippies started, I saw
some of them about and quickly decided that that was for
me. As soon as I left school in 1970, I began growing my
hair and wearing nothing but jeans. You could say that I
was fulfilling a childhood ambition. (Mick Parker)

Even before they had left school, it was frequently obvious which group fourteen and fifteen year olds would be
joining. Often, the type of music listened to was a reliable

indicator. Those listening to Pink Floyd or Simon and
Garfunkel would be far more likely to grow their hair and
smoke cannabis than they would be to shave their heads
and wear Dr Martens.

> In my class at school in 1969, you could see who was
> going to what once we left the following year. Some of the
> boys were already growing their hair a bit, while others
> were associating with older skinheads at the weekends.
> There were also plenty who were what some called
> 'straights'; meaning that they were going to be respectable
> citizens and probably go on to work in banks and so on.
> Whenever I bumped into any of my classmates a year or
> two after we had left, they had all turned out more or less
> as expected. (Mick Parker)

It must be noted that while there were many teenagers
affecting styles of clothing, length of hair and musical
tastes, which marked them out as having allegiance to
some subculture, these were still a minority of young
people. Most teenagers still left school, got jobs and were
all but indistinguishable from their parents' generation in
habits, mental attitudes and appearance.

Hippies

It was mentioned earlier that fashion in men's clothing
had remained pretty much the same from the end of the
First World War until the late 1960s – dark colours for
trousers and jackets, shirts with collars, ties worn generally during the day. Minor details of clothing might have
varied over the years, turn-ups on trousers for instance or

button-down collars on shirts, but the general appearance remained the same for over half a century. Together with this conservative approach to clothes went an absolutely rigid adherence to the correct length of men's hair – that is to say exceedingly short; the 'short back and sides' ruled for the first three quarters of the twentieth century.

> The trend for long hair among teenage boys began of course with the example of many pop singers in the sixties. Until 1970 or so it was restricted to a tiny handful of hippies, but the trend spread until by the end of the decade the teenager with the short back and sides was the exception. My own father regarded anything other than a ferociously short back and sides as being the thin edge of a very ugly wedge. One day you stopped having the hair on the nape of your neck shaved off by the barber with an open razor and the next you would be taking drugs and attacking police officers. It was, for him, an infallible indicator of degeneration. (Geoffrey C. Feldman)

> I don't think that teenagers change much over the years, not really. They always appear to have a knack for zeroing in on the thing which middle-aged adults, especially their parents, will really find annoying and likely to wind them up. In the early seventies, long hair was one of those things. Looking back, it was a fairly harmless thing to grow hair a bit longer than everybody else was doing, or, in the case of the skinheads, to shave it off entirely. Nothing drove older people (men in particular) wilder than seeing an eighteen-year-old boy with hair halfway down his back. Of course, it developed into a battle of wills between father and son. Most fathers at that time have been in the army, either during the Second World War or doing National Service, and long hair was utter anathema to them. (Martin O'Connell)

Short hair for men and boys was an absolute fetish until
the late 1960s, with long hair being widely equated with
artistic temperaments or moral laxity, depending upon
one's prejudices. Today, some teenage boys have short hair
and others long, but one rarely sees the classic 'short back
and sides' which held sway for much of the century.

> Until I was fourteen or fifteen, visiting the barber meant elec-
> tric clippers taking off my hair right up the back of by head.
> It was the only acceptable haircut for a schoolboy from a
> decent home. The year before I left school, in 1970, I had had
> enough of this and stopped going to the barber altogether. The
> reason was that 'short back and sides' was all that the average
> barber knew. It was no use asking a barber in those days to
> shape a man's hair or anything of that sort. It would have been
> regarded as rank effeminacy. You went to the barber to get a
> proper haircut and that meant extremely short. It led to end-
> less rows with my parents and also trouble at school. It was
> touch and go whether they would let me sit my GCEs without
> having my hair cut. This sounds so ridiculous now, but boys
> could be suspended from school for not having very short hair.
> (Christopher Walker)

> I cannot to this day understand just what it was about boys
> having long hair that used to make older men angry. I mean
> literally angry; they were furious at the sight of an eighteen
> year old with hair down to his shoulders. Among my circle of
> friends it was a very competitive thing, seeing who could grow
> his hair the longest! For many older people, any boy with long
> hair was automatically a drug-taking dropout. (Mick Parker)

Hippies, both boys and girls, rejected the clothing conventions of their parents. By the early 1970s, hippies were calling

themselves 'freaks' as often as they were hippies. This was a self-depreciating adoption of a derogatory term applied to them by the more conventional. Jeans became almost the uniform of the hippies, with girls also favouring ankle-length maxi skirts. Old army greatcoats for boys and Afghans for girls replaced the dull overcoats worn by their parents' generation. Clothing was freely swapped between the sexes; a thing which could never have happened in the past. Girls would borrow their boyfriend's jeans and men would think nothing of wearing an afghan or strings of beads.

My boyfriend and I were always swapping clothes. Tops and jeans were completely interchangeable and so were the strings of beads, pendants, scarves and so on. Some friends occasionally noticed that I was wearing jeans with the zip on the boys' side and would remark on it. It was all part of breaking down barriers between the sexes. From behind, it really was a case of not being able to tell which of us was the boy and which the girl. We would both be wearing tie-dyed vests and jeans. His hair was as long as mine, that is to say hanging right down his back. I know that it used to annoy older people and straights, but maybe that was part of the fun. (Polly Reynolds)

The great thing about being a 'freak' was that you could wear pretty much anything you liked. People forget how stifling the dress codes at that time were. 'Smart' meant a collar and tie for males and a dress or skirt for females. Trouser suits for women were becoming just about acceptable for 'smart' wear, but they had to be very smart indeed to pass muster. The whole thing with freaks was that the girls wore jeans a lot and the lengths of skirts was deliberately very different to those of our mothers' generation; very long, usually. A respectable girl wore a skirt with tan tights, but the freaks

often had bare legs when they were wearing a skirt. Shocking!
(Katherine Cassidy)

If you had seen me and my girlfriend from behind in 1971
you really would have had trouble working out which of us
was the boy and which the girl. We were the same height;
both wore either Afghans or old army greatcoats, jeans,
plimsolls and so on. Our hair was the same colour and also
the same length, hanging right down over our shoulders.
(Mick Parker)

This blurring of the divisions between the sexes enraged
some older people, as did the supposedly universal habits
among hippies of free love and the consumption of illegal
drugs. Whether it was because they feared that these young
people were enjoying life in a way that they had never been
free to do, due to the constraints of the 1930s economic
depression or the situation during the Second World War,
many older people seemed to feel a visceral hatred for hippies and everything for which they stood.

I am sixty now and I still can't understand why older
people became so angry at the way that I used to dress
in the early seventies. I don't mean that they were merely
irritated or thought we looked like idiots, which, of course,
was perfectly true. Many people used to be infuriated at the
very sight of us; the length of our hair, the clothes we wore,
our lifestyle. Everything about us seemed to wind up my
parents' and grandparents' generations. It's funny because
my own children dressed very oddly – one was a Goth – but
it never had the effect of making me angry! Older people in
the 1970s seemed to be furious at us, just because we didn't
want to dress and behave like them. (Anon)

Being a 'freak' meant looking scruffy and not appearing to care at all about one's appearance. Who wanted to abide by those outdated, bourgeois conventions? Our fathers wore ties and had short hair; very well then, we would never wear ties and we would grow our hair right down our backs. Most of what we did was based on a conscious effort to reject what 'straight' society stood for. Our unkempt appearance was the outward sign of this. By the time I was eighteen, which was in 1971, my hair was longer than my girlfriend's and I used to tie it back in a ponytail. I can't tell you how disgusted my father was. (Christopher Walker)

Hippies set out to challenge all aspects of conventional society, setting up instead their own vision for the future which became known as the 'alternative society'. Essentially, this meant turning away capitalism and its trappings and returning to a simpler lifestyle, where everybody would be able to do just what he or she pleased.

We really believed that we were building an alternative society, that we were forging a new kind of world. Capitalism was out and our own form of cooperative living was the way that things would be in the future. Unfortunately, our lifestyle was not a very good advertisement for this new way of life. I lived in a commune for about a year and it was impossible to get anything done, even the cleaning and shopping, without endless ideological debates. In the end, the girls used to get fed up with the dirt and so we drifted into a situation where the guys lounged around smoking dope and the girls did all the cleaning! (Mick Parker)

Male hippies were usually at least sixteen or seventeen; that is to say that they had left school, and if they were studying it was likely to be at a technical college. Female hippies, sometimes known as 'hippie chicks', were younger than that, sometimes even as young as fourteen or fifteen.

> When I was fifteen, I used to be a weekend hippy. I was at a very good girls' school, but on Fridays I would change into classic hippy style clothing and visit my boyfriend at the squat where he lived. It was fun, because at weekends and during school holidays I could play at being a freak with him and the other people at the squat. Most of the guys, who were I suppose about eighteen or nineteen, had girlfriends about my age. Sometimes there would be runaways there, girls who looked even young than me. There were some older girls that I used to see there, but I would say that the average age was no more than sixteen. (Polly Reynolds)

The practical incarnation of the alternative society preached by the hippies was the commune. This was a house which was either rented cheaply or squatted in. Such a place would soon fill up with many young people, most of them on benefits with the majority supplementing their income by means of shoplifting or dealing drugs. No questions were asked of anybody turning up at communes and as a result they typically became the haunts of runaway teenage girls and young people of both sexes who had left home because of disputes with their parents.

> When I was sixteen, I had a row with my mum and went to stay for a week at a commune in Hackney where my boyfriend lived. It was great! Everybody stayed up as late as they wanted; nobody bothered with housework or asked me what I was going to do when I left school. It was such a change from home. I did not stay for more than a few days

though. Part of the problem was that there was no hot water at all. This meant that the place was pretty filthy. Clothes had to be washed in cold water and don't even get me started on the state of the bathroom. There were quite a few houses like this at the time and they were supposed to be the thing of the future; communal living not based around the nuclear family. It was a great relief to change my clothes and have a hot bath when I went home. (Katherine Cassidy)

Communes gave the hippies an edge over other youth movements. Getting a place of one's own was impossibly expensive for most sixteen year olds, but one could turn up at a commune with a sleeping bag and be fairly confident of not being turned away. Living conditions tended to be squalid, because of course nobody had any duty or responsibility to clean, buy food or pay the rent. In practice, the occupants of communes tended to rise late and then spend much of the day smoking cannabis and listening to rock music. This lifestyle was enormously attractive to many teenagers because it was just what they wanted to do. Many had left home for precisely this reason; because their parents had objected to them lazing around all day doing nothing more strenuous than listening to Neil Young or Pink Floyd.

In 1972, I moved out of home and joined a commune when I was eighteen. I was there for nearly a year before the property was repossessed. I became terribly unhealthy during the time I lived there, because we didn't eat properly and smoked all the time. I was on National Assistance, which just about covered my day-to-day needs. Among the other occupants of the house were an army deserter, a thirteen-year-old girl who had run away from home, and two students who had dropped out of university. (Anon)

Teenage tribes often emerged in mutually antagonistic pairs. The hippies grew their hair long, wore extravagantly decorative clothes and believed in peace and love. Their antithesis was the skinhead movement, which began more or less contemporaneously with the hippies in the late 1960s.

Skinheads

Skinheads, in comparison to hippies, shaved their heads almost completely bald, courted violence and espoused extreme right-wing politics such as opposition to gay rights and a dislike of ethnic minorities.

> I have to admit, I did go down to Brick Lane with a bunch of friends in 1976 with no other intention than attacking some Asians. We used to call it 'Paki bashing'. It didn't turn out quite as we expected, because there were more of them there than there were us. In fact, some of the young guys whose fathers were running shops and so on ended up attacking us and chasing us down the street. (Anon)

> Most teenagers have always wanted to draw attention to themselves; dressing up in Dr Marten's and shaving our heads was just one of those things. I honestly don't think that most of us were really right-wing thugs. We used to get mixed up in fights on the terraces at football matches, but even that didn't come to much, just trading punches and kicks. I didn't know anybody who went out 'queer bashing' or anything like that. It was just fun to dress like a hard nut and know that people were a bit cautious of you. (Chris Arthur)

Whether the skinheads of the early 1970s deliberately set out to be the opposite of the hippies is impossible to say.

All we can say is that every aspect of their culture seemed to be diametrically opposed to the hippy culture. Hippies wore necklaces, pendants and beads; skinheads shunned anything that smacked of frivolous trappings. Hippy clothing was colourful, wild and extravagant; skinheads wore only neutral colours and their clothes were functional and drab.

> It all seems mad now, but all we looked forward to was punch-ups. A fair came to town one day and we couldn't wait to go. Not to go on the rides, but just so we could pick fights with the fairground workers. They were mainly gypsy types and they were only too happy to oblige. Attacking Asians did happen a bit, though I never did any of that. Our group once robbed a gay man, seeing him as an easy target. (Chris Arthur)

> We were dead against hippies. I don't know why now, except that they used to get on our nerves. We would sometimes roll a freak or turn over some squat if we couldn't think of anything else to do. They never fought back you see, just said things like, 'Hey man, that's not cool!' When you're that age you do have groups that are against your own. Sometimes it's supporting different teams, but in those days it was skinheads and freaks. When my brother was my age it had been mods and rockers. (Anon)

Standing a skinhead next to a hippy would show at once that these were two very different tribes. The clothes worn by skinheads tended to be pale fawns, browns and whites and were purely functional; braces to hold up their trousers, plain coats – even the heavy 'bovver boots' that they wore were fitted to their purpose of 'putting the boot in' during violent clashes. All this contrasted sharply with the bright colours and extravagant plumage of the hippies, for whom decoration and show were everything.

> We never wore any sort of decoration, except that it was OK for a guy to have an identity bracelet with his name on it. It's funny; I don't think I've seen one of those for years. You used to see the hippy types with the boys and girls both tricked out in all sorts. Headbands, beads, fancy shoulder bags, fringes sewn round the bottom of their jeans, embroidery, everything you can imagine. We felt our look was manly. All the stuff we wore had a purpose and that was it, nothing extra. (Chris Arthur)

The favoured drug of skinheads was alcohol and, unlike the hippies, they tended to eschew illegal drugs such as cannabis and LSD. There was, though, the same inclination to overdo their drug of choice. Getting drunk was popular with skinheads.

> I tried smoking dope once, but it didn't do anything for me. We used to get pissed at the weekend and the more we drank the livelier and more likely to get into a fight we got. From what I could make out, the freaks just got quieter and quieter when they smoked. My friends and I couldn't see the point of sitting round in a dark room listening to records all night. We wanted to be out on the streets, getting up to stuff. (Anon)

Even though both the hippies and skinheads rejected ordinary values (those held by the generation above them), the skinheads saw themselves as the upholders of a particular set of working-class values. Both groups indulged in criminal activity, although of very different kinds – hippies would steal from shops or defraud banks, insurance companies or the National Assistance without a second thought, justifying these thefts as a species of Marxist redistribution of wealth. The skinheads would also steal, but more often from individuals. They had their own rules though, that those who they stole from must belong to one of the groups they detested. Bursting into a hippy squat and stealing any money or drugs on the premises would have been quite acceptable and in fact happened on many occasions. Attacking gay men and stealing their money after viciously assaulting them was also thought to be a reasonable way of topping up one's finances. This activity was called 'rolling a queer'. Skinheads would descended upon areas known to be gay cruising grounds and attack and rob anybody who they thought looked likely to be gay. Asians were another target perceived as being fair prey.

> We used to like a bundle or fight with somebody who could stand up against us, like bikers, but if we wanted to go out on 'the rob' we always wanted easy targets. Gays were good because they would not go to the police. Some places, respectable businessmen used to go cruising and you could see at once that they would have fat wallets with them. Mostly, there was not much violence involved, as long as they just handed over their money; I think they were just scared of any trouble. (Anon)

> We might shout at people in the street that we didn't like the look of, gays or Asians say. OK, it wasn't very nice, but that was about the limit of it. We never actually went

for anybody, just called out, 'Oi, you queer bastard!' or
something like that. (Chris Arthur)

In contrast to hippies, who could be any age up to thirty
or so, skinheads were almost invariably teenagers. One
seldom saw a skinhead over the age of twenty. They
may have been aggressive hooligans, but this behaviour
declined sharply within a few years of leaving school. It
was not uncommon to see a hippy that still had shoulder
length hair well into their twenties, but you would not see
this with the skinhead haircut.

> A couple of years after leaving school, most of us had had
> enough of the skinhead thing. It's OK when you're fifteen
> to charge round looking for a fight, but once you have a
> girlfriend and that, it's not really the thing. It was a laugh
> while it lasted, but you grow out of it. (Chris Arthur)

There were both male and female skinheads, the girls wearing their hair short, although not quite as short as the boys.
This in itself marked them out as being disreputable in just
the same way as the long hair of the hippy males did. In the
early 1970s, short hair in a girl was unusual. The skinhead
girls could be as aggressive as their male counterparts, not
being at all averse to mugging hippy-looking girls or young
Asian women.

> We used to have a reputation ourselves for being hard. We
> didn't fight so much although that did happen sometimes.
> Maybe if some other girl was flirting with your boyfriend
> you might give her a smack. We used to like picking on
> people who looked soft. Hippy type girls, Asian girls,
> people like that. Sometimes we would nick things from

them, stuff like bits of jewellery. The boys used to like it, to
think that they had a girlfriend who was as hard as them.
It was the whole thing, making people scared of us. (Anon)

One of the defining characteristics, one might almost
say the *raison d'etre*, of skinheads was aggression. They
actively courted confrontation with those who they
disliked. Even if this did not always amount to physical
violence, there would be verbal harassment of minority
groups of whom they disapproved. The two most common
expressions used by these teenage thugs were 'aggro' and
'putting the boot in'. 'Aggro' is short for aggravation and
'putting the boot in' is self-explanatory. The skinheads
vanished in the early 1970s, to make a brief reappearance
ten years later, before vanishing forever.

Although I used to like the feeling that straights were nervous
of us, after a bit you get tired of it. Young men have always
liked to make a bit of themselves and parade about looking
tough, so I don't think being a skinhead was all that different
from what had always happened in areas like that where I
grew up. From what my dad and his own father told me,
young men in poorer parts of the city had always shown off
by picking fights and being horrible to outsiders. I suppose
that looked at in that way, we skinheads were just the latest
in a long line of young men wanting to prove their manhood.
(Chris Arthur)

Students

In an age where perhaps half of all teenagers go on to college or university, it is not easy to imagine a time when
students were a separate and fairly distinctive group

among young people. In 1970, fewer than 10 per cent of
young people went on to higher education. The 'Student
Power' movement of the late 1960s had created the
impression among many people that all students were left-
wing agitators. Many students affected the same clothing
as the hippies; indeed many of them *were* hippies. While
the hippies believed in peace and love, many students
were more politically conscious. They demonstrated and
marched on the streets, clashing with the police as they
protested about racism, gay rights, Vietnam and South
Africa; among other issues.

> I was at a technical college in 1970 and then went on to
> university two years later. I have to say, we fitted the stereo-
> type of students at that time. I hardly ever attended lectures,
> spent most of the time either smoking dope or protesting
> about South Africa. In fact, the popular image of students
> then – lazy, drug-taking and sexually promiscuous – was
> pretty well spot on, at least among my friends. The main
> thing I remember about being a student in the seventies is all
> the badges that we used to wear. We had them on our lapels
> like medals; Free Angela Davis, the CND logo, the clenched
> fist, GLF. It told people who you were; was a way of defin-
> ing yourself. At our college almost everybody had badges of
> various sorts pinned on their jackets or shoulder bags. You
> hardly ever see them these days. (Christopher Walker)

Before 1970, most teenagers who wished to go into further
education after the age of sixteen would stay on at school and
enter the sixth form; essentially remaining schoolchildren for
another two years. A trend developed, however, whereby
many such young people would reject this option in favour
of attending a technical college to do their A levels. The

old technical colleges, what we now call Further Education Colleges, were traditionally the sort of place where young people went to acquire practical skills. Now, they became a favourite stepping stone to university. Sixteen year olds who opted to go to a technical college rather than a sixth form were free to grow their hair long, wear whatever they wished and, most important of all, were not treated as children.

> When my older brother had wanted to study A levels, it was taken as a matter of course that he would stay on for the sixth form. When I turned sixteen in the early seventies, I did not for a moment consider going into the sixth. For one thing, it would mean keeping my hair short. I know this sounds pretty insignificant now, but it was a really big thing at the time. Besides, I had had enough of being a schoolboy; I wanted to be a student. There was a big difference. (Mick Parker)

> It will sound really strange, but my ambition at school was to be a student. They looked as though they lived such exciting lives. There they were on the television, battling the police on demonstrations, organising 'sit-ins' at universities like the London School of Economics, taking drugs, indulging in free love. As a respectable, middle-class schoolboy during the 1960s, it was all that I dreamed of and when I left school in 1970, I went straight to a college, followed by university – it was a dream come true. I could sit around all day talking revolution with other idealistic eighteen year olds and we could plan how we were going to overthrow straight society. (Christopher Walker)

Ostensibly, all those left-wing students who were so passionate about apartheid and the wickedness of the

American bombing of North Vietnam were polar opposites of the skinheads. In fact, they often shared a common love of mob violence. Skinheads were viewed as pack animals that would only attack their victims when accompanied by a crowd of like-minded fellows. So too were a lot of the students from technical colleges and universities. For some, their true nature and desire for excitement and brawling became increasingly clear as the 1970s progressed and the National Front became more prominent.

> At demonstrations, the students were sure to be at the heart of any trouble. I suppose that we thought of ourselves as the vanguard of the proletariat, as Lenin called them. It was our job as intellectuals to give the lead and we saw attacking the police as being the first stirrings of the revolution which many of us longed for. I say attacking the police, but it mostly amounted to chucking cans and stones at them. We often came off worse, because they had horses and truncheons. If we were arrested then the only sensible thing to do was plead guilty, because in those days the magistrates took the police's word for everything and enjoyed coming down hard on rowdy students. (K.A. Silverstone)

Whenever the National Front arranged a demonstration, students were sure to be there in force; on the face of it to oppose the National Front, but in reality to vent their hatred of the police. Police injuries at such events were invariably caused by students and left wingers, many of who seemed to have no interest in attending such marches other than attacking the police. Just as many skinheads relished battles after football matches, so too did some students enjoy the excitement of throwing bottles and bricks at police officers and creating mayhem and disorder.

I can admit, at this late stage, that part of the attraction of demonstrations, those against the National Front in particular, was the chance of violence. I was at Red Lion Square in 1974 when a student was killed, and also at Lewisham three years later when the police first used riot shields. These were heady days and as a politically conscious eighteen year old who would not have dreamed of vandalising things or beating people up, those protests were an outlet, a source of excitement. The chanting, the confrontation with the lines of police, chucking bottles and bricks, it was absolutely thrilling. We did not admit it, even to each other, but I am sure that for many of us the hope at such events was always that they would descend into chaos and violent disorder. (Polly Reynolds)

Bikers

This was a group or subculture which was exclusively male. There were hangers and camp followers who did not necessarily own motorbikes of their own, but bikers themselves were all young men. Of course the cafés and pubs where bikers hung out would be especially attractive to girls who found this scene enticing. Because being a biker entailed actually owning a motorbike, the average age of the members of this group tended to be a little older than that of the skinheads, for example. After all, a boy of fifteen could dress up in skinhead gear at the weekend, but a youngster of that age would not be able to afford, nor would it be legal for him to ride, a Harley-Davidson.

I was a biker bird, as we used to call ourselves. The bikers were the most exciting of the young men in our town. The skinheads were kids, the hippies looked like a bunch of soft

things, but the bikers were real men. The fact that everybody tended to be a bit wary of them and not cross them
was also part of the attraction; that and the fact that every
adult heartily disapproved of them, of course. For a lot of
girls, and I was one, there has always been a fatal fascina-
tion for bad boys. Why would you go to the pub with a
bunch of straights wearing collars and ties, when you could
instead be in the company of leather-jacketed tearaways
who smelt of engines? (Gillian V. Pettitt)

Despite their reputation for being uncontrollable and wild,
most bikers really wanted only to tinker with their machines
and see who could exceed the speed limit by the great-
est margin. That is not to say that bikers did not become
embroiled in fights and disorder, but that they did not in
general seek out such things. They were resolutely apoliti-
cal, being interested only in their chosen hobby. One would
be unwise to insult or otherwise antagonise a biker because
they would be unlikely to back away from a fight, but they
did not go seeking trouble. It was possible to walk past a
group of bikers without the fear that they would fall upon
anybody who was not a member of their particular group.

We didn't go out of our way to get into fights, but on the
other hand we wouldn't back down from one either. Speeding
along little country roads was the main thing and outwitting
the police if they tried to stop us. If anybody did want trouble, we certainly let them have it. (Martin O'Connell)

When I was at school, I saw a film on TV called *The Wild
One*. It had Marlon Brando in it as a biker, who led a whole
gang which terrorised a town in America. They didn't
actually do much; it was more that everybody was nervous

of them. I knew that that was what I wanted to be. The girls in the film were all dead impressed by the guys on the motorbikes and that was another reason why I took to the idea. (Anon)

Female members of this subculture were called 'biker birds' and they could range in age. The police were more tolerant of bikers than they were of hippies, skinheads or students. While some other tribes often went out of their way to attack other people, the bikers were more likely to harm themselves than anybody else. The sight of a one-armed or one-legged former biker was not particularly uncommon; these being the sort of severe injuries liable to be sustained in high-speed collisions.

I knew one guy who only had one arm. He lost the other one in a smash-up. I used to ride behind my boyfriend and was only involved in one accident, which was when I was seventeen. This would have been at the end of 1976. It wasn't really anybody's fault, he just skidded and I came off the bike. I had grazes all over the place; what we called 'road rash'. When my parents saw it they went absolutely mad. Being a mother myself now I can well understand why they were so angry. They probably were thinking that I could have ended up on a slab. They still had some influence over me, because I was still living at home and the upshot was that I didn't go out with that boy again. I suppose the truth is that I had been a bit shaken up myself by the accident and wasn't that keen on getting on the back of his bike again anyway. (Theresa O. Littlestone)

Being the parent of a biker or one of their 'birds' produced stomach-churning anxiety in a way that was seldom the case with the mothers and fathers of hippies and skin-heads. With these groups, parents might worry that their sons or daughters might be arrested for drugs or brawling in the street, but for those whose teenage children were connected with bikers, the fear was that they might one day answer a knock at the door and find a policeman standing there with news that their child had been killed in a road accident.

> My boyfriend was a biker and he used to take me out to various meet-ups. These would often be in some little pub or roadside café in the middle of nowhere. Obviously, we got there on his bike. We used to race along those country lanes at a completely crazy speed and I used to shout at him to go faster. My mother used to suffer agonies, worrying about what would happen if there was an accident, but I was nineteen and there wasn't much she could do to stop me going out. My favourite record by a mile was 'Leader of the Pack', which was all about a girl whose boyfriend was a biker. (Gillian V. Pettitt)

The bikers were probably the smallest of the teenage tribes of the 1970s, but they were certainly noticeable. In the early 1960s it was quite the thing for the bikers, known then as 'rockers', to descend on seaside towns and wreak havoc by fighting with other youths, but that sort of thing died out around 1965. Throughout the 1970s, the bikers simply got on with riding their bikes; they scarcely bothered anybody.

> I had a bike from 1975 onwards, when I was nineteen. I used to hang round with other bikers, mainly in a few roadside cafés out of town, rather than pubs. In all that time I don't remember us doing anything other than tinkering with

our machines and racing each other along deserted roads
at night. True, this could be a nuisance and perhaps even
a danger to others on the road, but nobody ever got hurt
by our actions. One or two friends had accidents and one
guy I knew was killed a few years later, but that was after
I had stopped riding. In general, it was like a club where
teenagers and young men in their early twenties hung around
and talked about motorbikes. Some places wouldn't allow
people in who were wearing leathers, a few pubs were like
that, but apart from that nobody disliked us that I knew of.
(Martin O'Connell)

Teenyboppers

If the vast majority of bikers were male, then teenyboppers
were invariably female. They ranged in age from ten to
about seventeen and typically became obsessed with certain
young pop singers; usually those who sang soulful ballads.
The archetypal objects of their affections were androgynous
boys like David Cassidy and Donny Osmond.

For my birthday last year, my husband bought me a compendium of *Jackie*; the magazine we all used to read. There
was a picture in it of David Cassidy and I was struck by how
much like a girl he looked. I can't think that we used to have
any sexual desire for him; it was purely a crush type thing.
I know that we used to swoon back in 1973 at the thought
of kissing him, but I don't believe any of us ever thought of
being in bed with him! He really doesn't look like a male at
all, more like a teenage girl himself. (Sarah P. Moran)

The thing to bear in mind about the teenybopper idols
is that while all the other singers and bands were doing

drugs and screwing around, the biggest teenybopper
band, the Osmonds, would not even drink tea or coffee
because they were too stimulating! They were unbelievably wholesome, the sort of young men that your parents
would be happy for you to be going out with. This was
part of their attraction. You would feel safe if Donny took
you out. (Maria T. Valentine)

Most pop music could be appreciated by any age and
was seldom just for males or females. Music favoured by
teenyboppers, however, was not listened to by anybody
who was not either a girl, or under the age of eighteen.
Cults developed around the singers upon who crushes
were developed, with posters and memorabilia being
religiously collected.

Even now, forty years later, I can remember the aching
feeling of being in love with Donny Osmond. I knew absolutely everything about him, every detail of his childhood,
background, tastes, the whole lot. My bedroom was like
a shrine, with posters, magazines, records, anything at all
to do with Donny. I remember his song 'Puppy Love'. It
summed up perfectly how I felt: 'And they called it puppy
love, just because we're in our teens. I guess they'll never
know, how the young hearts really feel'. Whenever I was
tempted to dismiss some craze of my daughter's when she
was growing up, I used to remember that song and it made
me think twice and try and put myself in her place, think
about how it felt to be thirteen. (Mary A. Barker)

Most of the groups at which we have so far looked had distinctive tastes in music, but also other unifying features. In
the case of the teenyboppers, music was the only thing which

defined the group. By definition, teenyboppers were those young girls who were fans of particular singers or groups.

> Having crushes on the Bay City Rollers or David Cassidy was something that only you and your friends could be involved in. It was like a trial run for being in love. You could fantasise about these boys without any danger. There was no chance of rejection because you were never going to meet them anyway, nor would you be pressurised into doing anything disgusting. This was a pure love, free of anything overtly sexual. You thought of going on a date with them, perhaps even kissing, but certainly nothing more than that. It was a bit like being in a secret society, one which excluded your parents or anybody else who was not female and about twelve. (Maria T. Valentine)

Perhaps the archetypal teenybopper group was the Bay City Rollers. Formed in Scotland in 1966 as The Saxons, the band chose a new name by the simple expedient of throwing a dart at a large map of the United States and taking as the name of their band the nearest place to the dart; which happened to be Bay City, Michigan. Reaching their peak popularity around 1974, the Bay City Rollers were compared by some to the Beatles. Over forty years after breaking up though, one still hears Beatles songs regularly. It is somewhat rarer to hear anything today turned out by the Bay City Rollers.

Forty years later, it is hard to grasp the adoration in which teenybopper idols were held by their fans. There is certainly no parallel in modern terms. These young men were not so much admired, as worshipped. Across the country, teenage schoolgirls would chant in playgrounds mantras such as the following:

B-A-Y, B-A-Y,
B-A-Y, C-I-T-Y,
With an R-O double L, E-R-S,
Bay City Rollers are the best!
Eric, Derek, Woody too,
Alan, Leslie, we love you!
With an R-O double L, E-R-S
Bay City Rollers are the best!

Against such madness there was little that parents and teachers could do except wait for the craze to subside.

There are still equivalents to the teenybopper singers of the 1970s, but there is not the frenzied adoration that was such a notable feature of the 1970s. You might get fans hanging round a place where a singer is expected to put in an appearance, but we no longer see the hysterical mobs of girls under the age of seventeen who besieged hotels and airports, screaming and fainting.

I remember in 1973, David Cassidy came to London and his hotel was surrounded by adoring fans, of which I was one. The average age was probably thirteen or fourteen and they had converged on the hotel from all over the country. The police were very kind about it all, but it must have been a ter-rible nuisance to them. And the screaming when he actually appeared; there is not the least doubt in my mind now that we were all in the grip of a mad hysteria. It took over everything for some girls, to the extent that they could not sleep at night or concentrate on their schoolwork. I never had it that bad, although my bedroom was like a shrine to the guy, with post-ers and pictures cut from magazines and all sorts of other junk. (Mary A. Barker)

Punks

The punk scene did not appear until halfway through the 1970s. It was closely associated with a style of music, typified by groups like the Sex Pistols. Visually, punks set out to shock; their hairstyles were deliberately bizarre and they adopted such things as razor blades, safety pins and bondage gear for decoration, making a statement that they rejected conventional values. In some ways, they were similar to the hippies, although their opposition to ordinary society was more aggressive.

Being a punk was great. You could say or do anything at all, no matter how revolting, and it was all excused because that was what punks did. I didn't always feel like having a bath and I used to smell a bit, but hey, that was fine; I was a punk. I was rude to people, got pissed and threw up in awful places, but that was fine; I was a punk. You could dress as outrageously as you wished, be as foul mouthed as you liked and if anybody objected then it just showed how many hang-ups they had. Being a punk in the seventies was like being a caricature of a teenager. Most teenagers behave a little oddly and dress in ways which their parents don't like, but with the punks, this was taken to extremes. A lot of what we did and the way we dressed could almost have been designed to upset and annoy people. I don't think that this was what was going through our minds, but that was definitely the effect it had on old people. I mean, why shave the sides of your head and then grow the bits in the middle, the way that some of my friends did when they grew what was known as a mohican? It was almost as though somebody had sat down and thought, well the hippies wound people up with their long hair and the skinheads annoyed people because they shaved their heads. Why don't we devise a hairstyle which is a combination of the two; part shaved and part ridiculously long? (Mary A. Barker)

The punks were rather like a post-modernist youth culture, which took bits and pieces from all the other teenage tribes and stuck them together to make a mocking statement about youth. Some wore the leather jackets of the bikers, others wore hippy style clothes. Some grew their hair long; others shaved it off like skinheads. Having utterly thrown out the traditions of adult society, they went on to refuse to be associated with any of the previous teen groups. We saw that most teenage sub-groups of that time had earlier incarnations; the hippies sprang from the beatniks, the bikers from the rockers and Hell's Angels. The punks, though, seemingly appeared from nowhere, a completely new group of young people, completely different from any seen previously.

As soon as I became aware of punks some time in the mid-seventies, while I was still at school, I just knew that these were the people for me. They looked so completely different from anybody else and, best of all, they didn't seem to care about anything. Swearing was something that we all avoided doing too much in public or in front of our parents, for instance. The punks though, they seemed to be swearing all the time. I remember I was watching *Today* with my parents in 1976 when Johnny Rotten was on it. Bill Grundy more or less let him say and do what he pleased and he began effing and blinding like nobody's business. My mother was so upset about hearing those words, but it seemed to me that he was saying something important about people being delicate and too easily offended. A year later, once I had left school, I too was swearing like a navvy all over town. (Mary A. Barker)

In comparison to the hippies and the students who were embodying a cause, the punks were essentially nihilistic. They were simply opposed to what decent middle-aged people held dear; older people were offended by bad language? Great! Let's have a record called 'Never Mind the Bollocks, Here's the Sex Pistols.' Just leaving the album cover laying around will be enough to upset your parents, as it not only has the word 'sex' on it, but another, even less acceptable word!

> There was an awful lot of swearing. What you need to bear in mind is that words like f*** and so on were far less acceptable in the seventies than they are now. It is not at all uncommon these days to be watching the television and for a character in a drama to swear, but at that time it was almost unheard of. Punks used this squeamishness about strong language to make a point, that traditional society attached too much importance to words alone. (Paul Clarke)

Straights

It is perhaps unfair to describe straights as a sub-group of teenagers. These are young people who simply continued to dress and behave much as their parents had for generations. They dressed 'normally', did not experiment with illegal drugs or fall foul of the police. They studied or went to work and were indistinguishable from people in their twenties or thirties. These are the teenagers who got engaged, often married young and saved up for a house or put things away for a bottom drawer. To some adults, they showed that not all young people were dropouts, drug addicts or hooligans. Looking at these respectable

and responsible teenagers acted as a counter to all the
newspaper stories suggesting that there was a generation
gap. There was, for the majority of the older generation,
something reassuring about these youngsters.

> I just followed my father into the same factory without even
> thinking about it. I used to go to the pub with him, meet
> his friends and stay home a lot in the evenings, watching
> television with my parents. When I fell in love with a girl, it
> seemed the most natural thing in the world to get engaged
> and then marry her. I suppose that my life in the seventies
> was pretty much identical to my parents' lives in the for-
> ties. I certainly didn't have any inclination to grow my hair
> down to my shoulders or shave it all off or dye it pink or
> anything. I liked my parents' way of life and couldn't see
> any reason not to follow it myself. (Geoffrey C. Feldman)

> None of my friends dressed weirdly or took drugs. We just left
> school and lived normal lives. When you look at photographs
> from the seventies, you sometimes get the impression that all
> teenagers were punks or skinheads or something. It wasn't
> like that at all. Of course, there were people my age who took
> up with the Hare Krishna people or who joined communes,
> but most of us didn't. You hear a lot about the generation gap
> as well, but mostly teenagers got on all right with their mum
> and dad. It's true that fashions changed during the seventies
> and that men stopped wearing ties so much, but this was not
> radical. I think most people simply left school and behaved
> very much as their parents had done. (Esther M. Hannigan)

Among the teenage subcultures at which we have been
looking, 'straight' was used as a pejorative term. It suggested somebody boring and respectable; somebody who

lived a dull life. Hippies originally coined the expression to describe 'ordinary' society. Groups of teenagers who were discussing some other teenager known to them, who they regarded as being unadventurous and following in his parents' footsteps, might perhaps say, 'Oh, he's a real straight'. The old beatnik word 'square' meant much the same thing. A straight was not 'with it'.

> I never really got any of the youth movements that were popular when I left school. I hated motorbikes, did not want to shave my head or grow my hair halfway down my back, nor did I want to become a student. I just wanted to get a job in an office, save up, buy a place and get married. My own impression is that most young people were like me, or at least there were more like me than there were skinheads or hippies. Nearly all the people in my class at school got normal jobs and lived in much the same way that our parents had done. We liked different music and were more likely to sleep with our girlfriend before we were married, but our general lifestyle was hardly distinguishable from our parents. When you see pictures of young people from the seventies, they always seem to be skinheads, Hell's Angels, hippies and so on. In fact, the vast majority were pretty much like their parents. (David Ford)

There were other connotations to being straight. If a group of bikers or hippies were discussing anything at all dodgy, from fiddling benefits to shoplifting or taking drugs, they might caution against letting somebody else hearing of the matter, on the grounds that he was straight. A straight would not do anything dishonest and possibly could not be relied upon to keep his mouth shut about it if he heard others planning something illegal.

I could never see anything particularly clever about stealing from shops or using drugs. Nor did I see much point in
dressing up in odd clothes so that people would stare at you
in the street. I knew after I left school in 1975 that some of
the people from my class had become hippies and others
punks. They would take the rise out of me if we met in the
pub, because I still dressed the way that I did when I was at
school, that is to say wearing a collar and tie and keeping
my hair short and tidy. Sometimes they would stop talking
if I was nearby and I guessed that this might be because they
had been talking about something illegal like drugs. I know
that they thought I was a straight and as such not really to be
trusted. I wasn't that bothered because I was earning twice
as much as any of them within a couple of years of leaving
school. There was something to be said for just knuckling
down and getting a steady job. (Geoffrey C. Feldman)

In our bunch we often used to call people straights.
We weren't bikers or freaks or anything like that, but we
used to spend a lot of time in pubs, smoke dope and get
up to stuff that wasn't really legal. 'Straight' was a handy
way of warning people you were with that they should not
mention too much to somebody. It was a slur as well. If you
baulked at some mad scheme, your mates might have said,
'Oh, you're such a straight!' Now we didn't use the word so
much about older people, our parents' generation. We more
or less took it for granted that they were straight. Instead,
we reserved it for those of about the same age as us; those
in their late teens who thought and acted in a conventional
way. (K.A. Silverstone)

The ironic thing about the straights is that they probably
comprised the great majority of teenagers throughout the

whole of the 1970s. Because hippies, skinheads and bikers were so noticeable, it would be easy to assume that all teenagers in the 1970s were behaving outrageously and spending most of their time at pop concerts, demonstrations against the war in Vietnam and so on, but this was not at all the case. The default setting for teenagers forty years ago was 'straight'.

> From time to time I would see pictures of hippies and protesting students in the paper, but none of this had much to do with me and the life I led. I knew that these people existed, but not only did I not belong to one of these groups, neither did anybody that I knocked around with. There is a very famous image from around 1977, which is of a young punk with a pink mohican. I genuinely never saw any teenager with a hairstyle even approaching that. I'm not saying that there weren't any, but if there were, then they must have been pretty rare. Perhaps you had to go to the King's Road in Chelsea to catch sight of this sort of youth. Nearly everybody I knew was what some referred to contemptuously as 'straight'. (Pat Howard)

Photographs and news reports from the time can be horribly misleading. There is something newsworthy about a bunch of students smashing things up during a demonstration. Similarly, a punk with an outrageous hairstyle has got to be worth a picture for the newspaper. Such images became iconic and for many people define teenagers in the 1970s; the student, the punk, the skinhead and so on. As has always been the case, a lot of history stems from the media's portrayal of that time, and the iconic images and news stories create a very particular view of the 1970s.

While talking about the seventies, I raked out a picture taken of myself in 1975. It was taken one weekend and I am wearing a tweed sports jacket and collar and tie. In those days, some places would not let a man in without a tie, but in any case this was how I usually dressed if I was going out for the afternoon or evening. I must have been nineteen at the time that this picture was taken. What strikes me is that nobody would have thought that this was a typical representative of teenagers of that time. It wouldn't have made a very good icon of the seventies; a young man wearing a sports jacket! And yet if you walked down the street, there was far more chance in most places in the country of coming across a teenage boy looking like that than there was of finding a punk or hippy. (Geoffrey C. Feldman)

When I was ten, I remember seeing pictures in the newspapers of the mods and rockers fighting at Margate. I remember being fascinated because I had never seen any mods or rockers in real life. My parents clucked disapprovingly about it all, but as far as I could gather from their conversations they too had never actually set eyes on a mod or a rocker! Exactly the same thing happened in the 1970s. The papers were full of pictures of protesters, punks, and various other types, but all that most of us actually saw were ordinary teenagers who were just going about their business in an ordinary and unremarkable fashion. They weren't rioting, they weren't taking drugs or going to pop concerts, nor were they dressing in outrageous and flamboyant styles. You would pass the average teenager on the streets and they would more than likely look like a younger version of their mum or dad. (Mick Parker)

On my way to the office each morning – we lived in a London suburb and I commuted to the city – I would see many young people of about the same age as me; seventeen or eighteen year olds. The boys, like me, were wearing collars and ties, the girls wore conventional skirts, with flesh-coloured tights. All in all, we looked just like our fellow commuters, some of whom were thirty or forty years older than us. The only difference might be that our ties were slightly brighter or we might have a different style of suit. This was in the mid-seventies and it struck me, even at the time, that the sixties revolution and the permissive society seemed to have passed many of us by. We were going to work like everybody else, saving up to get married or engaged, hoping to buy a house of our own one day. We might have loosened up at the weekends, but our general lifestyle was very conventional. (Anon)

Although the 1970s will be remembered for its teenage sub-cultures, the vast and overwhelming majority, though, just as with today's teenagers, lived normal and unremarkable lives; going to work or school, coming home and having tea, watching television, going shopping and seeing friends.

We all define the seventies by certain images. Old-fashioned looking Bobbies with traditional helmets battling students or strikers, punks with their hair sticking up, things like that. You could just as well have had images of ordinary teenagers going off to work or sitting quietly in a pub planning an engagement party. I bet there were more types like that than there were all the punks, hippies, skinheads and all the others put together. (Polly Reynolds)

If you enjoyed this book, you may also be interested in …

'You've Never Had It So Good!'
Recollections of Life in the 1950s
STEPHEN F. KELLY

The 1950s saw a major shift in the lifestyles of many in Britain. The austerity that had dogged the 1940s after the end of the Second World War began to give way to better times. Employment levels rose to new heights, television replaced the radio in most homes, rock and roll was born, leisure time increased, families went on holiday, and the new Queen was crowned — bringing in a glorious new Elizabethan age. Including interviews with former Labour leader Lord Neil Kinnock, footballers Bobby Charlton, Wilf McGuinness and Terry Venables, among others, this delightful compendium of reminiscences will appeal to all who grew up in this post-war decade.

978 0 7524 5996 7

A 1950s Housewife
Marriage and Homemaking in the 1950s
SHEILA HARDY

Being a housewife in the 1950s was quite a different experience to today. After the independence of the wartime years, women had to leave their jobs when they married and support their husband by creating a spotless home, delicious meals and an inviting bedroom. *A 1950s Housewife* collects heart-warming personal anecdotes from women who embarked on married life during this fascinating post-war period, providing a trip down memory lane for any wife or child of the 1950s. This book will prove an eye-opener for those who now wish they had listened when their mothers attempted to tell them stories of the 'old days', and will provide useful first-hand accounts for those with a love of all things kitsch and vintage.

978 0 7524 6989 8

Visit our website and discover thousands of other History Press books.

www.thehistorypress.co.uk